TWAYNE'S WORLD AUTHORS SERIES

A Survey of the World's Literature

GUATEMALA

Luis Davila, Indiana University

EDITOR

Rafael Arévalo Martínez

TWAS 544

Rafael Arévalo Martínez

RAFAEL ARÉVALO MARTÍNEZ

By MARÍA A. SALGADO

University of North Carolina at Chapel Hill

TWAYNE PUBLISHERS

A DIVISION OF G. K. HALL & CO., BOSTON

Copyright © 1979 by G. K. Hall & Co.

Published in 1979 by Twayne Publishers,
A Division of G. K. Hall & Co.
All Rights Reserved

Printed on permanent/durable acid-free paper and bound
in the United States of America

First Printing

Frontispiece photograph of Rafael Arévalo Martínez

Library of Congress Cataloging in Publication Data

Salgado, María Antonia.
Rafael Arévalo Martínez.

(Twayne's world authors series ; TWAS 544 : Guatemala)
Bibliography: p. 135-37
Includes index.
1. Arévalo Martínez, Rafael, 1884-   —Criticism
and interpretation.
PQ7499.A7Z87   863'.6'2   78-32085
ISBN 0-8057-6387-2

To Liane and Danny

Contents

About the Author

María A. Salgado was born in the Canary Islands (Spain). She graduated with honors at Florida State University in 1958, received her M.A. from the University of North Carolina at Chapel Hill in 1960, and completed her Ph.D. at the University of Maryland in 1966. After teaching at Maryland for one semester, she moved to Chapel Hill, where she is now Professor of Contemporary Spanish and Spanish American Literature.

Ms. Salgado is the author of a number of articles and reviews dealing with several aspects of twentieth-century literature, published in Hispanic and American journals. Her major works to date include *El arte polifacético de las "caricaturas líricas" juanramonianas* (Madrid: Insula, 1968) and *¡Hablemos! Textos contemporáneos para conversar o escribir* (New York: Harper and Row, 1976).

Preface

It is not easy to write an introduction to the complex world of Rafael Arévalo Martínez. Arévalo's literary production spans a period of more than sixty years. His first public recognition came in 1909 when he won first prize in a short story contest held by the magazine *Electra*, and his last book was published in 1971. In the course of his career, the writer matured and felt the influence of several literary movements, a fact reflected in the variety of themes and styles contained in his complete works.

In order to understand his many works, one must know something about his life and cultural milieu. Hence, this book begins with an introductory chapter on his life, time, and general literary background. The subsequent chapters discuss his creative works according to genre—poetry, novel, and short story.

Contemporary critics are almost unanimous in their agreement that Arévalo Martínez is primarily a poet, and yet they are also unanimous in avoiding an evaluation of his contribution as a poet. This study seeks to correct that lack. In Chapter 2 I have analyzed his poetry and shown through the study of his major themes, as well as the most salient traits of his style, how Arévalo's poetry progresses from a very artificial, modernistic pose adopted in his early poems to a mature, simple poetry that reflects his growing concern for basic human values.

Arévalo Martínez made his most lasting contribution to Spanish American literature in the field of the narrative. Kessel Schwartz considers his psychological works the beginning of the new novel. Ironically, the attraction of today's narrative is at times so powerful that few critics have had the time or the inclination to study the works of the precursors and to examine the painful development of a tradition in a continent where little fictional literature was produced before the twentieth century. I have grouped Arévalo Martínez's novels around three unifying themes that show his development from an introspective obsession with himself to an awareness of the social problems that surround him. Hence, Chapter 3 studies the psychological novels, works that deal mainly with the interior life of the protagonist-narrator, obviously an alter ego of the author; Chapter 4 discusses Arévalo's growing concern with the discouraging social situation in Guatemala and his corresponding involvement; finally, Chapter 5 examines a further step in Arévalo's awareness of mankind's problems: his utopian novels reveal his concern for the situation of the world and offer alternatives and guidelines that might improve economic conditions and bring peace to the planet.

Students of Spanish American literature know Arévalo Martínez as the author of one single work, the short story "The Man Who Looked Like a Horse." With it he introduced a new type of narrative called the psycho-zoological tale. Chapter 6 studies these and other types of stories and analyzes the importance of his creation. The relevance of his contribution to Hispanic letters is examined in the final chapter.

An exhaustive and definitive analysis of all of Arévalo Martínez's works and a complete biography and bibliography are beyond the scope of a volume like the present one. This study is intended rather as a general survey and an introduction to his life and works. For more detailed studies of specific points, the reader is directed to the selected bibliography at the end of this book. I have quoted critical opinion when it contributes significantly to the understanding of his works or when it is at odds with my conclusions. All translations are my own, and a number of them are rather free renderings. The reader is warned that it is difficult to do justice to a writer and a poet as preoccupied with style as Arévalo Martínez. Those with a knowledge of Spanish are urged to consult the originals.

In closing, I wish to express my gratitude to the Research Council of the University of North Carolina at Chapel Hill for a grant that made possible a trip to Guatemala. There I had the pleasure of meeting Don Rafael, who most generously made available to me some hard to find works and who graciously answered all my questions in reference to his life or to his own opinion as to the significance of his works. I am also indebted to my colleagues Frank Domínguez and Frank M. Duffey for their constructive criticism and their careful reading of the manuscript.

MARÍA A. SALGADO

University of North Carolina at Chapel Hill

Chronology

1884	July 25: born in Guatemala City, the oldest child of Rafael Arévalo Arroyo and Mercedes Martínez Pineda.
1892–1902	Studied at the Colegio de Infantes.
1911	Published his first book of poems, *Maya*. Married Evangelina Andrade Díaz, by whom he had seven children, four boys and three girls.
1912–1920	Worked as reporter and editor for several periodicals, including his own short-lived *Juan Chapín* (1913–1914).
1915–1920	Member of the staff, and later editor, of *Centro América*, official publication of the International Central American Office.
1914	Published his first autobiographical narrative, *Una vida (A Life)*, and a second book of poetry, *Los atormentados (The Tormented)*.
1915	Published his best known work, *El hombre que parecía un caballo . . . (The Man Who Looked Like a Horse)*.
1918	*Las rosas de Engaddi (The Roses of Engedi)*, his third book of poems, appeared.
1920	Made his first trip to the United States. The false news of his death was spread throughout the Spanish-speaking world.
1921	Named corresponding member of the Spanish Royal Academy of the Language.
1922	Published *Manuel Aldano*, a second autobiographical novel, and *El señor Monitot (Mister Monitot)*, a collection of short stories.
1925	Published *La Oficina de Paz de Orolandia, novela del imperialismo yanqui (Office of Peace in Goldland, Novel of Yankee Imperialism)*.
1926–1945	Served as director of the National Library of Guatemala.
1927	Published his fourth novel, *Las noches en el Palacio de la Nunciatura (Nights at the Palace of the Nunciature)*.
1933	Published his third collection of short stories, *La signatura de la esfinge (The Sign of the Sphinx)*.
1934	Published *Llama (Flame)*, his fourth book of poems.
1939	Issued the first of his utopian novels, *El mundo de los*

	maharachías (The World of the Maharachías), and its sequel, *Viaje a Ipanda (Journey to Ipanda)*.
1940	Published *Los Duques de Endor (The Duke and Duchess of Endor)*, his first drama.
1943	Published two essays: *Nietzsche el conquistador (Nietzsche the Conqueror)* and *Influencia de España en la formación de la nacionalidad centroamericana (Spain's Influence in the Formation of Central American Nationality)*.
1945–1945	Published *¡Ecce Pericles!*, a biography of the Guatemalan dictator Manuel Estrada Cabrera, and was named delegate to the Panamerican Union in Washington, D. C.
1947	Published his fifth collection of poems, *Por un caminito así (Through a Path Such as This)*, and *Hondura (Depth)*, his seventh novel.
1954	Published one of his most important essays, *Concepción del cosmos (Concept of the Universe)*.
1955–1956	Traveled through France, Switzerland, Italy, and Spain.
1956	Published a second drama, *El hijo pródigo (The Proddigal Son)*.
1958	Published *Poemas (Poems)*. Awarded the Great Cross of Rubén Darío (Nicaragua's highest honor) and the Order of the Quetzal of Guatemala for his literary and poetic works.
1959	Published *Obras escogidas, prosa y poesía: 50 años de vida literaria (Selected Works Prose and Poetry: 50 Years of Literary Life)*, on occasion of his fiftieth anniversary as a literary figure.
1960	Published his eighth novel: *El Embajador de Torlania (The Ambassador from Torlania)*.
1965	Published two anthologies of his own poetry: *Poemas de Rafael Arévalo Martínez (Poems by . . .)* and *Poemas (Poems)*.
1968	Published the autobiographical *Narración sumaria de mi vida (Brief Narration of My Life)*, and *Cratilo, y otros cuentos (Cratylus, and Other Stories)*, his fourth collection of short stories.
1971	Published *4 contactos con lo sobrenatural y otros relatos (4 Contacts with the Supernatural and Other Tales)*, a collection of stories and personal notes.
1975	June 12: died in Guatemala City.

CHAPTER 1

The Man And His Times

I Historical and Literary Background

GUATEMALA, the birthplace of Rafael Arévalo Martínez, is a
country whose very name conjures up visions of Maya ruins
amidst exotic jungles. Its trademark is variety: "This lush, beautiful,
sprawling country has mountains with steaming or sleeping vol-
canoes; sloping highlands and deep valleys, abundant crops growing
in their rich soil; coastal lowlands, covered with wet, luxuriant
jungles of forest giants; deep-blue, mirrored lakes and rushing
streams; attractive towns—charming, ancient Spanish towns with a
rich patina, and shiny, new modern ones."[1] Under all that beauty,
however, lie violence and turmoil. Tragedy is a way of life; it is always
present, hidden by deceivingly simple bucolic scenes, played out
against a background of majestic landscapes. The most persistent
national tragedy has been political instability. During most of
Guatemala's history, her national government has been very cen-
tralized, autocratic, and arbitrary. Despite the provisions of the
several constitutions the country has had, presidents have served as
veritable dictators, ruling with varying degrees of force, and conduct-
ing the affairs of government in their own way without bothering
much either with the written provisions of the constitution or with
what political opponents have to say. The army and the police have
been used to enforce the commands of the president, while the
people have been kept uninformed and under strict control. Hence,
there have been few political disturbances, and peace and order have
tended to prevail.[2]

From a literary standpoint, political oppression has created an
atmosphere that has curtailed freedom and discouraged experimentation and dynamic artistic creation. The unbelievably cruel reign of
terror that the dictator Manuel Estrada Cabrera (1875–1924) brought
upon the country during the years of Arévalo Martínez's youth would

be re-created by him in *¡Ecce Pericles!* (1946), a biography of the tyrant. This same historical figure inspired another Guatemalan, the Nobel Prize winner Miguel Angel Asturias (1899–1974), to compose his masterful novel *El señor presidente* (1946).

Estrada Cabrera was a tyrant, but he fancied himself a liberal and a patron of the arts. Under his rule, Guatemala became for some years the focal point of intellectual activity in Central America, due more to the lack of centers of higher learning in the neighboring republics than to the dictator's efforts. But he did subsidize many famous foreign poets, among whom Rubén Darío (Nicaragua, 1867–1916), José Santos Chocano (Peru, 1875–1934), and Porfirio Barba-Jacob (Colombia, 1883–1942) were the best known.

Despite Guatemala's intellectual dominance in Central America, its literary development, at the turn of the century, had fallen behind that of the most progressive Spanish American countries. Nineteenth century movements still were the norm: writers in the Romantic and *Costumbrista*[3] veins continued to grind out a steady stream of outdated historical novels, regional tales, and *cuadros de costumbres.*[4] In contrast, in most other Hispanic countries, a new and vigorous movement had taken hold, introducing changes that would eventually put an end to the intellectual dependency on Spain. This new movement was *Modernismo,* which in its broader implications was not restricted to Spanish America alone. According to the Spanish critic Federico de Onís, it represents rather "the Hispanic form of a universal crisis of letters and the spirit that initiated around 1885 the dissolution of the nineteenth century and that was to manifest itself in the arts, science, religion, politics, and gradually in all aspects of life."[5]

Guatemalan literature, controlled as it was by nineteenth century schools of thought, did not show the first manifestations of Modernism until the opening years of the twentieth century. The writers who traditionally have been credited with introducing the new movement to Guatemala are Enrique Gómez Carrillo, Rafael Arévalo Martínez, and Máximo Soto-Hall. In most other Spanish American countries, on the other hand, Modernism had been established much earlier by another generation of artists whose main concern was the renovation of a stale literary tradition. These writers believed that, although political independence from Spain had been achieved in most countries over half a century earlier, artistically Spanish America was still a colony. Dissatisfaction with what was considered to be the dominance of peninsular literature and the tyrannical rule of the Spanish Royal Academy of the Language was prevalent. The search for self-knowledge and an original American expression was initiated about the middle of the nineteenth century. The works of such early writers as Domingo Faustino Sarmiento (Argentina, 1811–1888), Ricardo Palma (Peru, 1833–1919), and Eugenio María de Hostos (Puerto Rico, 1839–1903) already show the discontentment that continued to spread and eventually culminated in the works of the *Modernistas*. This movement ultimately succeeded in creating a Spanish American consciousness and in developing a sense of pride in the artistic achievements of the young nations.

From the standpoint of the development of poetic movements in Spanish America, Modernism appeared at the outset as an immediate reaction against Romanticism. The passion that had characterized the early poetry of this period had turned to empty rhetoric by the 1880s. The Cuban poet and patriot José Martí (1853–1895) was the first Spanish American writer to turn toward a form of expression that emphasized a greater control of the emotions. His book *Ismaelillo*, which was published in 1882, marks the beginning of Modernism. Most literary historians agree that, besides Martí, there were at least three other writers who helped in the renovation and who make up the first generation of Modernists: Manuel Gutiérrez Nájera (Mexico, 1859–1895), Julián del Casal (Cuba, 1863–1893), and José Asunción Silva (Colombia, 1865–1896). These writers, although working independently, shared a common concern for the creative process and a desire to search for new avenues of expression. As a result of their efforts, Modernism was born.

The definition of Modernism is highly controversial. Literary critics have argued about it for almost a century without achieving consensus or conclusion. Today two schools of thought seem to prevail. For one, the most widespread and traditional in its approach, Modernism is reduced to a simple literary school, identified with very precise characteristics and narrowly limited in time, from the date of Rubén Darío's *Azul* (*Blue*) in 1888 to roughly the time of the death of this poet in 1916.

The Chilean critic Raúl Silva Castro is one of the most passionate defenders of this concept. He lists the following characteristics as identifying marks of the school:

1. elaboration of form,
2. search for new poetic meters and rhythms,
3. elegance,

4. opposition to prosaic vocabulary and approach,
5. exoticism,
6. use of fantasy,
7. art for art's sake, and
8. pervading sensuality.[6]

This list shows that for Silva Castro, as well as for the many other critics who concur with his interpretation, Modernism is a rather inconsequential movement, associated with a literature of exoticism, decadence, and escape. These indeed are marks of Modernism; they can be used to characterize certain aspects of Darío's work and certainly stand out as its most readily identifiable features. But limiting the characteristics of the movement to its most obvious and superficial aspects misrepresents the scope of the revolutionary role it played in the development of Hispanic letters.

The second school of thought, which has gained acceptance slowly but persistently as new research has demonstrated the deep changes of attitude heralded by Modernism, sees it as a multifaceted movement, one which certainly includes the characteristics presented above, but which reaches far beyond them. Critics such as Federico de Onís, Juan Ramón Jiménez,[7] Ricardo Gullón,[8] and Ivan Schulman,[9] among others, have carefully researched the available evidence and propose that Modernism is not a literary school, but rather an "estilo de época" (epochal style) as pervasively influential as the Renaissance or the Baroque were in their times.

Ivan Schulman blames Rubén Darío's self-praise and the fact that he proclaimed himself the founder of Modernism[10] for the confusion of the critics.[11] For Schulman, Modernism started before Rubén Darío and continued long after his death, proceeding through a series of evolutions that he considers characteristic of this dynamic movement: "Modernism is a continuous progress toward American maturity and self-discovery and in the art of the Modernist writers one finds a succession of modalities, norms, and, at the same time, cyclical analogies of attitude and style."[12]

Such a complex movement does not lend itself to easy definitions. It can perhaps best be explained as being characterized by the spirit of the times it represented. According to Schulman, "The spirit of the epoch is one of protest and escape from the spiritual vacuum created by the weakening of norms and traditions brought about by positivism and the new experimental science. The artist feels alienated from a bourgeois culture which tries to convert him into a mediocre instrument, into a captive being. . . . In order to preserve his creative freedom the artist had to create an 'escape' culture and to live in it."[13]

The escape from reality and the building of private worlds resulted in a highly individualistic concept of art and in a proliferation of styles and approaches which responded not to any objective or external pattern, but rather to the subjective needs, the temperament, and the will of each creative artist. With this proliferation, the aesthetics of the movement became increasingly multifaceted and contradictory, making practically impossible a definition by any one set of characteristics.

Regardless of the definition one may choose for the term Modernism, there is no doubt that its followers shared many traits. In the literary manifestations of the movement, two factors were important in Spanish America: a reaction against Spain, and a receptiveness to the influences of other literatures, especially the French. The *Modernistas'* rebellious mood prevented them from basing their renovation of Spanish American poetry exclusively on Spanish models. Instead they searched for inspiration in foreign sources and found it mainly in French Parnassianism, Symbolism, Impressionism, and even Romanticism.[14] The Romantics had experimented with new rhythms and verses, but the Modernists truly revolutionized poetry by shattering the old concepts of metrics. Traditional verse measures disappeared, opening the way, among other things, for the successful adaptation of free and blank verse. New stanzas, new meters, and new word and rhyme combinations also produced dramatic results. The Modernists, however, did not limit themselves to the creation of new patterns; they also resurrected, and brought up to date, every verse form ever used in Spanish poetry. The result of all this activity was a change of such proportions that it has often been compared to the profound transformation undergone by Spanish verse in the Golden Age in the hands of Garcilaso de la Vega, Herrera, and Góngora.

Yet, no matter how important this formal renovation may have been, it was not an end in itself; rather, it was symptomatic of a change in sensibility and the consequent desire to express new attitudes. The predominant feelings among early Modernists were doubt and disenchantment, which resulted in anguish, ennui, and all the pessimistic emotions associated with *mal de siècle*. Discontent with their milieu, many experimented with drugs or dabbled in mysticism and the occult, while many others escaped into worlds of fantasy. Evocations of Greece, eighteenth century France, and the Orient became common poetic motifs. To re-create these private worlds, the poets developed a carefully wrought language, which made use of a great number of symbols of elegance borrowed from the plastic arts—swans, . peacocks, fleurs-de-lis, lotuses, jewelry, enamels, and gems made their poems sparkle with beauty.

Another characteristic of early Modernism is the use of colors and music, a borrowing from Symbolism. One of the lasting contributions of the movement, the systematic incorporation of synesthetic images in the poetic language, came about through the experimental fusing of sound and color. When the French poet Arthur Rimbaud said in his sonnet "Voyelles" ("Vowels," 1871), "A black, E white, I red, U green, O blue . . ."[15] he succeeded in provoking a sensation of color by using as stimulus a sound, and vice versa, and opened up a treasure chest of sensorial possibilities, which were fully exploited by the Modernists. Most of the experimentation took place during the initial phase of the movement. For some poets, it culminated in artificial refinement and a *preciosista* cult of form, while others went on to utilize the artistic gains of the group to express, in a personal and lyrical style, transcendental questions dealing with the eternal mysteries of life and death, and still others worked toward the development of an American consciousness, their goal being to capture the spirit, the ideals, and the hopes of the Americas in their art. The result of all this activity and variety was a vitality never before present in Spanish American literature. Thanks to Modernism, a home-grown movement, the young nations finally gained confidence in their creative abilities.

Rafael Arévalo Martínez, a Modernist in the broadest sense of the word, creates his own aesthetic world. Literary historians who have forgotten the anarchic nature of the movement have been faced with insurmountable problems when they have tried to classify his writings within the narrow limits of a specific literary school. Thus, for Luis Alberto Sánchez,[16] Arévalo belongs to the school of Imagists; for Luis Leal,[17] he is a post-Modernist; for Enrique Anderson Imbert,[18] a Modernist; for Hellén Ferro,[19] a Surrealist; for Graciela P. de Nemes,[20] a precursor of Absurd literature; and for Kessel Schwartz,[21] a precursor of Magic Realism. I believe that a thorough analysis of his works and thought proves without a doubt that he is above all else a Modernist, a creator of a highly original world, endowed with the new sensibility to which Federico de Onís refers and concerned with the search for aesthetic goals characteristic of the movement.

II *Formative Years*

It has been said that literary fame and glory depend not only on the genius of the artist himself, but also on the circumstances that surround him and the historical moment in which he was born.[22] Rafael Arévalo Martínez was born with a weak constitution, and he grew up in a country that had little to offer from a literary standpoint. However, he became a prominent and influential literary figure in spite of these handicaps. He has always been painfully aware of his unusual circumstances and has referred to them repeatedly in his works, especially emphasizing the problems of those who must try to create in a literary vacuum resulting from their country's sparse intellectual life:[23]

The work of art is half in itself, the work itself. The other half is the human element that receives it. Here, as in the rest of the world, there are the subject and the object; the spectacle of the creation and the spectator, who is man. Here among us [in Guatemala] one can say that the spectator is missing, that is to say, that the work is mutilated.

La mitad de una obra de arte es ella en sí misma, la obra de arte en sí. La otra mitad, es el elemento humano que la recibe. Aquí, como en el universo, hay el sujeto y el objeto; el espectáculo de la creación y el espectador, que es el hombre. Aquí entre nosotros   [en Guatemala] puede decirse casi que falta el espectador; es decir, que la obra queda mutilada.

And later on he adds, ". . . it is necessary to have a true poetic temperament and to be truly strong in order to elude and to conquer this hostile environment" ("se necesita tener un verdadero temperamento de poeta y ser de veras fuerte para sustraerse a este ambiente hostil y vencerlo").[24]

The absence of a reading public and the resulting lack of constructive criticism are adverse circumstances with which Arévalo Martínez had to contend practically all of his life. Thus, though encouraged by family and a small group of enthusiastic and understanding friends and driven always by his great faith in himself, he found the creation of a significant and truly universal body of writings a most difficult and demanding undertaking.

From the moment of his birth the odds seem to have been stacked against him or against his success. Rafael Emilio Arévalo Martínez, born in Guatemala City on July 25, 1884, was the oldest of six children. His early years set the pattern for his later life. His nearsightedness, precarious health, weak constitution, and chronic neurasthenia prevented his having anything near a normal childhood.[25] To make matters worse, the atmosphere of his home was conspicuously austere and melancholy.[26] As the years passed, nothing changed significantly in his personal circumstances or surroundings. Thus, his adolescence and his adulthood represented a continuation of the unhappy situation of his childhood. Physically, for example, the weak, homely, and wistful child simply grew into a weak, homely, and pensively melancholy man or, as he described himself years later, "a cadaverous, tall, thin poet, wearing glasses for myopia" ("un poeta cadavérico, alto, delgado, con anteojos de miope").[27]

During his childhood, life was relatively comfortable. Don Rafael Arévalo Arroyo's law practice allowed him to support his family in relative comfort, but his severity of character created a barrier that prevented young Rafael from becoming truly acquainted with his father. In contrast, the boy was extremely close and devoted to his maternal grandmother and, especially, to his mother, Mercedes Martínez Pineda. Doña Mercedes was a sad, sweet woman of great integrity who was fond of repeating to her children the proverbs and maxims that form the basis of the uncomplicated, wholesome ethos of the common people. It was his mother who molded his character, instilling in him strength and moral rectitude. Arévalo Martínez's close relationship with his mother is confirmed by his daughter, Teresa Arévalo, who says that for every conversation Don Rafael held with his father he had one hundred with his mother, whom he loved passionately. She taught him to respect women, to be honorable with men, to live by high moral standards, and to love truth above all.[28]

At five and a half years of age, Rafael started attending kindergarten, together with his younger sister, playmate, and accomplice, María. The impact of this school, and later of the "Colegio de Infantes," on the young boy is narrated in his autobiographical story *Una vida: novela corta* (*A Life: A Short Novel,* 1914). Here one sees the fears, frustrations, and tensions, as well as the triumphs, experienced by the child during his impressionable growing years. His first success in school was learning to read, an art he mastered in two weeks, after he realized that letters combined to form words and that

these in turn would eventually combine to tell stories. This fascination with reading continued through almost his entire school career
and came close to being his undoing. He would much rather read
than study, and he was constantly deceiving his teachers by hiding
books of fiction behind his textbooks. According to his own account,
he spent seven years at the "Colegio de Infantes" in the following
fashion: the first five as an extremely poor student, reading all the
time, in class, in bed, and even during meals and recess, followed by
another two years of unbelievably hard work in order to catch up and
to prove his worth to his family.[29] He succeeded in gaining its respect
during his last year at the "Colegio" by finishing at the head of his
class and winning ten silver medals. The effort, however, was more
than his weak constitution could take: Rafael became ill, and the
family doctor forbade his ever returning to school again; he made
resumption of study tantamount to a death sentence. As a result of
this diagnosis, Arévalo Martínez's formal education came to an abrupt
end in 1902, when he was eighteen.

During the following years, the young man was to experience all
the inevitable frustrations associated with the effort to survive in a
utilitarian society without formal training or profession and without
the strength to cope with the demands of regular daily employment.
Arévalo narrates these agonizing experiences in another autobiographical work, *Manuel Aldano* (1922). After several miserable attempts at working as a clerk in a general store, a bookkeeper, and a
bank teller, he finally accepted that he was unsuited for manual work,
a circumstance that had already been twice indicated by his doctors,
who described him as a "superior degenerate,"[30] suffering from
neurasthenia and incapable of concentrating on anything alien to his
morbid personality.[31] His physical weakness and his inability to hold
a well-paying job gave him a deep sense of insecurity and reinforced
his sense of failure. By the standards of a male-dominated society,
which placed a high premium on physical strength and virility, he was
absolutely worthless. In the novel *Manuel Aldano*, Don Rafael refers
repeatedly to his sense of inadequacy and to the strong death wish
that overwhelmed him every time he considered the humble and
unrewarding work he was forced to accept.[32]

Once Arévalo Martínez accepted the fact that he was unemploy-
able, he felt free to devote all his attention to furthering his literary
career, which had been launched successfully in 1909, at the height of
Modernism, while he was still employed as a teller by the Banco
Agrícola. This first venture into the literary world had won him first

prize in a short story contest held by the magazine *Electra*, for a composition entitled "Mujer y niños" ("Wife and Children"), submitted under the pseudonym Placencio Artigas. This same year of 1909, the Peruvian poet José Santos Chocano returned to Guatemala and quickened the enthusiasm of all the young writers and particularly that of Rafael Arévalo Martínez, who visited him at the hotel in which the politically amoral poet was the honored guest of the Guatemalan president, the dictator Manuel Estrada Cabrera. Arévalo's enthusiasm for Santos Chocano's poetry is seen in the fact that he asked him to write the prologue to his first collection of poetry, the book *Maya* (1911), published one month after his wedding to Evangelina Andrade Díaz.

Evangelina, a young girl known to family and friends as Eva, became the person who, after his mother, had the most beneficial influence on Arévalo. Significantly, they were married after a very short engagement, six months after the death of Doña Mercedes. Rafael had met Eva when she was only eight years old. He was nineteen at the time, and a frequent visitor at her house, where many of his friends lived as boarders. Eight years later they fell in love, and the sixteen year old bride found herself married to an "older man" of twenty-seven. The marriage was destined to be a very happy and rewarding experience for both of them—they lived together for over sixty years, building a home and sharing in rearing seven children and many grandchildren. His family responsibilities had a steadying influence on Arévalo Martínez's life. He normalized his working habits, held several teaching positions, worked on the editorial staff of *La República*, and eventually founded his own literary magazine, *Juan Chapín* (1913–1914), and edited the periodical *Centro América*. At the same time, he steadfastly pursued his own literary career, publishing new books at regular intervals. His life was so unpretentious and his work so modest that there was little surprise or disbelief when the false news of his death spread throughout the Hispanic world in 1920. Arévalo Martínez humorously commented that this incident afforded him the rare pleasure of reading his own necrology and seeing what his contemporaries thought of his works. He remained "deceased," for the literary world, until 1928, when the Spanish critic Federico de Onís announced to the world the "resurrection of Arévalo Martínez."[33]

As time went on, his life, which had never been particularly active, became more and more sedentary and completely dedicated to literature. In 1926, he became director of the National Library of

Guatemala and remained at that post for almost twenty years. Practically the only interruptions in his routine way of life were the year spent in Washington, D.C., as delegate to the Panamerican Union (1945–1946) and another year of travel with his family through Spain and other European countries (1955–1956). Almost all his living was done through his books, to the point that it is hard to separate autobiographical and fictional elements in his prose—to study his works is to know the man. The well-known critic Carlos García Prada tells a pertinent and revealing anecdote in this regard. Upon first meeting the writer, he asked him about his life. Don Rafael's answer was: "—My life? . . . What is important is written in my works. There is nothing in them that is not intimately related to my own experience" ("—¿Mi vida? . . . Lo que importa escrito está en mis obras. En ellas nada hay que no tenga íntima relación con mis propias experiencias").[34] He repeatedly emphasized the uneventfulness of his biography and on one occasion summed up his long life in the following fashion: "As for biographical data, I can only say that I was born in 1884, I got married in 1911, I have seven children, an unbelievably slight body (I weigh ninety-four pounds), chronic neurasthenia since age fourteen. And that is all" ("En cuanto a datos biográficos sólo le puedo decir que nací en 1884, que casé en 1911, que tengo siete hijos, un cuerpo endeble hasta lo inverosímil (peso 94 libras), una neurastenia crónica desde los 14 años. Y nada más").[35] Since everything worthwhile that ever occurred to him is recorded in his written work, the best way, if not the only way, to know the man and to evaluate his contribution to Spanish American letters is to analyze his works. This task will be undertaken in the remaining chapters of the present study.

CHAPTER 2

The Poet of Sincerity and Simplicity

RAFAEL Arévalo Martínez gained instant recognition in 1915 with the publication of his short story "El hombre que parecía un caballo" ("The Man Who Looked Like a Horse"). From that date on he has been acclaimed as one of the outstanding innovators of the contemporary Spanish American narrative. Paradoxically, and in spite of his acknowledged contributions to the development of prose, literary historians unanimously agree that Arévalo Martínez is primarily a poet. The critic Santiago Argüello has gone as far as to say, "I believe that in Guatemala there is no poet who is as true a poet as Rafael Arévalo Martínez."[1] Prose and poetry are inseparably united in every one of his creative works; the imaginative treatment of both is characteristic of his style, and it is also what marks him unmistakably as a Modernist. Practically all writers associated with this movement have been poets who, by dealing with prose in the subjective manner traditionally reserved for poetry, succeeded in creating highly artistic works of lasting value.

The development of Don Rafael's poetry follows a path similar to that of most Modernist writers.[2] His first works are characterized by a *preciosista*[3] style, best exemplified in the book *Maya* (1911). The poems in this collection abound in many of the excesses for which this type of early *Modernista* poetry has often been criticized: plastic images, elegance of vocabulary, and symbols of beauty and refinement.

"En las joyerías" ("In the Jewelry Stores") is a typically *preciosista* poem. The jewels become symbols of the beloved's beauty. The poet wonders if they have been taken away from her by some malevolent gnome: blue sapphires (eyes), red rubies (lips), gold rings (blond tresses), and silver cups (neck and bust), lie in the jewelry stores, scattered through the glass cases.[4] All images point to a beautiful but cold young woman, symbol of the frivolous, eternal female flirt,

24

protagonist of so many *preciosista* poems. The Guatemalan critic
Hugo Estrada L. includes in his analysis of Arévalo Martínez's poetry
a comparison of the Modernist traits of Darío and Arévalo. His
comparison of Rubén's "Era un aire suave . . ." ("It Was a Soft
Tune . . .") and Arévalo's "Bizantina" is very revealing. He shows
how both poets use the same metric form (the melodious dodecasyl-
labic line) to deal with essentially the same topic (woman's flirtatious
spirit); both create the same general atmosphere by emphasizing
similar images and similar sensations.[5] The analysis shows clearly that
in the opening years of his literary career, Arévalo consciously
emulated the works of Darío, the Modernist poet par excellence.

Another *preciosista* trait, the penchant for making allusions to
exotic places and elements, appears in several compositions, as, for
example, in "El sueño del poeta pobre" ("The Dream of the Poor
Poet"). Here Arévalo refers to luxurious furs such as ermine and
marten, crystal from Hungary and Saxony, and porcelain from Japan
(*Maya*, p. 17). There can be no doubt that the author's purpose in the
poetry of this book was to create an atmosphere of sensual refinement
and aristocratic aloofness. Some of the same *preciosista* characteristics still persist in his second book, *Los atormentados* (*The Tormented*, 1914). In it, however, there is a timid move toward a new and
simpler poetry. Poems such as "Retrato de mujer" ("Portrait of a
Woman"), "Navidad" ("Christmas"), or "Sensación de un olor"
("Sensation of a Smell") already show a definite change toward a more
personal and simpler style.

Las rosas de Engaddi (*The Roses of Engedi*, 1918) is a book of
transition. Here the poet establishes the change toward the simplicity of style and tone that will be the rule in his mature works—*Llama*
(*Flame*, 1934) and *Por un caminito así* (*Through a Path Such as This
One*, 1947). A similar evolution can be found in the works of the most
important Modernist writers. In Spain, Antonio Machado (1875–
1939) and Juan Ramón Jiménez (1881–1958), and in Spanish América,
Rubén Darío (1867–1916), Amado Nervo (Mexico, 1870–1919), and
Enrique González Martínez (Mexico, 1871–1952), to mention only a
few, became less *preciosista* as they perfected their techniques. Each
of these writers consistently tried to rid his poetry of excessive
ornamentation and unnecessary rhetoric, aiming at creating poems of
intense feeling, expressed in more direct, simple images.
Modernismo's lack of rules allowed each of them to develop quite
differently; thus, by the time they reached artistic maturity, it was

hard to see them as members of a common movement. Yet they are all, in a sense, Modernists, engaged in their own individual search for self-expression and self-realization.

In a similar manner, Rafael Arévalo Martínez, midway in his career, put aside his elaborate early style and began to search for a simpler and more direct expression. This process of "de-ornamentation" is what Juan Ramón Jiménez called "desnudar la poesía" ("denuding poetry"). Juan Ramón's concept took him along the road of *poesía pura* ("pure poetry"), however, and his ideas on the streamlining of poetry are quite the opposite of Arévalo's. Juan Ramón looked for a purity which, like that of the French poet Paul Valery, was exclusively an artistic device, a means to allow him to find the essence of Beauty, synonymous for him with poetry, and, eventually, God. Arévalo Martínez, on the other hand, moved away from rhetorical and artificial elements simply to allow the poem to come forth more directly, giving the impression of unaffected spontaneity. The key word in his search was not purity, but rather, sincerity. In the last poem from the book *Por un caminito así,* he says:

> I will tell you the rules I follow:
> First of all
> to be sincere
> with God, with men and with myself.
> Second to be lucid, lucid and pure.

> Yo te diré los cánones que sigo:
> Es el primero
> de todos, ser sincero
> con Dios y con los hombres y conmigo.
> El segundo es ser claro, claro y puro.[6]

It is evident that the most important thing, according to Arévalo, is to be sincere. Purity is relegated to second place and carries, within the context of this poem, the meaning of simplicity and directness.[7] The purity sought by Juan Ramón Jiménez, on the the other hand, produced a hermetic poetry, detached from reality, which Don Rafael ridiculed in his poem "Poesía pura" ("Pure Poetry"):

> A flower without roots in the earth,
> is the desire of he who wishes
> to compose a pure poem,
> without walls to confine it,

> With mind and passion always at war,
> pure expression is pure folly

> Una flor sin raíces en la tierra,
> eso pretende todo aquel que ansía
> componer una pura poesía,
> sin la cárcel del vaso que la encierra,

> Con la pasión la mente siempre en guerra,
> pura expresión es pura tontería.[8]

This practical attitude has allowed Arévalo to contribute to an important change in Spanish American poetry: by concentrating on the creation of a poetic world in which common, everyday situations and objects are endowed with a lyrical dimension, he helped to give impetus to a movement which would bring poetry back to earth where it could deal with man's real problems.

The process of simplification in his poetic works, the manner in which he succeeds in creating a direct, almost prosaic expression, can be followed step by step by analyzing the presentation of his favorite themes during different stages of his literary development. In 1965, Arévalo published, under the title *Poemas de Rafael Arévalo Martínez* a collection of his best work, including some poems written after 1947, the date of his last previously published volume (*Through a Path Such as This*). The most prevalent themes in this anthology are woman, art, life, home, and religion; they will be used as the basis for an analysis of the development of his poetry that will demonstrate that, between 1907 and 1964, he attained his goals of simplicity and sincerity.

I *Woman*

Arévalo Martínez reserves for his poetry his most sincere and intimate feelings. This characteristic of his lyric works is never more evident than when he deals with the theme of woman. This particular theme was one of the favorite topics of Modernism. The treatment accorded to this subject by different poets ranges from the exaltation of exotic and decadent heroines, frivolous French courtesans, and fairy tale princesses to the exaltation of woman as the means by which the poet may transcend his physical limitations.

Don Rafael's attitude toward women has always been one of respect and admiration. His strong attachment to his grandmother, mother, and wife is easy to verify even from a quick glance at his biography, and it is reflected in many passages of his works. Respect for the women in his life gives his literary creations an intimate, sincere tone which is markedly different from that of other Modernist writers. In almost all cases, he endows his female protagonists with love, compassion, and strength of character. The treatment of woman in his poetry reveals that, basically, Arévalo has always respected her role in society as wife and mother. In many of his early poems, the author sees woman as an abstraction whose beauty and mystery capture the imagination. Yet, in some of these same early poems he pays homage to the conventions of decadence and erotic allusion. In "Mi amigo vino a tomar el té" ("My Friend Came to Have Some Tea"), he wonders if the protagonist is Cleopatra, Helen, Lady Godiva, or Salome, or if she is a heroine from myth or legend; the brunette beauty of "Bizantina" is a flirtatious girl with a wicked heart; and the protagonist of "Belleza" ("Beauty") is compared to a glass of heady red wine. In most poems, however, even during his early *preciosista* period, he concentrates on descriptions and images that emphasize woman's basic goodness and purity. In "La baldosa sin vida" ("Lifeless Paving Stone"), the woman imparts her life and warmth to something as cold, dead, and prosaic as a paving stone. In "De ella" ("Hers"), typically *Modernista* symbols of purity such as lilies, pearls, and orange blossoms caress, kiss, and adorn the persona.

Arévalo Martínez soon left aside this *preciosista* pose and began to assert his own thinking, especially the concept that woman is the embodiment of love and security. This belief was to become more pronounced as he grew older, slanting his love poetry not toward fire and passion, but rather toward the expression of deep affection and understanding. The faces of his mother, wife, and children can be imposed on the protagonists of many of his poems. In one of his best and most often quoted works, "Retrato de mujer" ("Portrait of a Woman"), he sings of a fat and ugly girl whose happy disposition brightens all the lives she touches. She is sister and mother to all who need her, and she fills the poet's life with peace and stability. This poem, written in 1914, already has all the characteristics associated with his mature works: in it he sings to a nonpoetic subject (a fat and ugly girl) and uses prosaic images (she is compared to the village's cows, her arms are like the handles of an earthen jar, she mends the poet's life and spreads it out in the sun) to create a moving and lyric portrait of the ideal motherly woman (*Poemas*, p. 16). Another poem that praises similar attributes of womanhood is "Ropa limpia" ("Clean

Clothes," 1921). Here Arévalo resorts again to simple images taken from everyday life (soap, clean clothes, new clothes, clear water) to delineate the portrait of a young, innocent girl (*Poemas*, p. 15). Her purity is indicated by a series of prosaic images of cleanliness, rather than by utilizing the more traditional and elegant imagery of lilies and orange blossoms. "A los pocos meses" ("After a Few Months") emphasizes that love is a product of *trato* ("familiarity"), not of beauty: the essential femininity of any woman can make a man forget her less redeeming qualities. Ultimately, the poet says, he finds himself in love with every woman with whom he is associated (*Poemas*, p. 18). Again, it is not the glamorous aspects he praises, but the sense of everyday stability and security that women provide. The ability to create an aura of serenity is to him one of the most charming and attractive qualities of womanhood.

In many of the poems of *Through a Path Such as This* (1947), Arévalo Martínez memorializes his wife, Eva, his constant companion of over sixty years. It is not difficult to discover her thinly veiled identity in the protagonists of many of his poems. "¿Para qué?" ("What For?") is an extremely short and moving poem in which the author acknowledges that he has remained alive only because his loved one asked him for a present. But, he wonders, when she is no longer here to ask, what will be the purpose of living? (*Poemas*, p. 34). In "¿Qué te parece de un pintor?" ("What of the Painter?") he comments that, as the painter needs colors for creating his paintings, he needs the inspiration provided by his beloved's eyes. He feels that every work he creates belongs to both of them, because he finds his worlds of make-believe in the depths of her green eyes (*Poemas*, p. 35). This is an extremely touching admission of what Eva's love has represented through the years—she had made everything possible by providing inspiration, which probably means that she has offered the security and support Arévalo always needed in order to create. Perhaps the most moving homage to his wife is the poem "Balada del amor maduro" ("Ballad of Mature Love"), where he touchingly exalts the comfortable, strong bond of love and understanding that binds lovers in old age. He explains in a series of simple stanzas the affection and contentment generated by the mere presence of his "vieja compañera" ("old comrade"). He also recognizes that the kind of love they share has become possible only with old age, for in earlier years they were too busy living, or as he puts it, the wine press of life would have rejected them as two bunches of green grapes, not ripe enough to make wine (*Poemas*, p. 28). Now the time has come, the spirit is ageless, and this moment becomes eternal. The simple language and musicality of the ballad create in the reader the same serenity with which the poet faces life in old age, secure in the love of his wife Eva.

II Art

This section of *Poemas* contains Arévalo's reflections on art and the role of the poet. As would be expected, he emphasizes the natural aspect of art and his desire to express himself without the restraint of preconceived ideas or grammatical rules. He exalts the role of the poet and the exhilaration of the creative act.

In his early poems, Arévalo Martínez optimistically sees himself as capable of the act of creating, in spite of difficulties that others may think exist. In the poem "Empeño" ("Persistence," 1909), he expresses his determination and success in capturing poetry. He presents this idea by combining a rather violent hunting scene (in which he chases rhythms, ideas, and images with hounds and hawks) with a more literary image in which he writes of patiently chiseling stone and a laborious study of dictionaries (*Poemas,* p. 60). It is this combination of hard, careful work and inspiration that will earn him his reward—the finished poem, captive on the page. In "Brochazos" ("Strokes of the Brush") another poem written in 1909, we find his preference for a simple poetry already formed. His simile presents the artist as an ordinary house painter, because, he says, nature paints its landscapes with thick strokes; his works will not be precisely delineated, but they will be natural "as a rose grows full of thorns" ("como llena de espinas crece la rosa"), he says, in a poetic image closely reminiscent of some of Juan Ramón Jiménez's ideas on pure poetry.[9]

Poems of later years show the characteristic streamlining of images in the interest of simple, direct expression of ideas. "Transparencia" (1914) expresses this tendency, as he explains his concepts rather directly, without the dressing of images or metaphors. He symbolizes the deornamentation process that his poetry is undergoing by describing the madness that moves him to disrobe in order to become as transparent as crystal (*Poemas,* p. 52). In short, the idea of a poem should not be obscured by rhetorical devices. This symbol also parallels other concepts expressed by Juan Ramón in reference to the importance of denuding poetry of excessive ornamentation.[10]

In "Creación" (1914), Arévalo describes the exhilaration of the creative act, using, once more, a very direct language. He likens poetic creation to the trauma of pregnancy and refers to a masculine urgency that accompanies the feminine tenderness he feels while composing:

> I felt a male urge
> and feminine tenderness
> and I begot in violence
> and I conceived in gentleness
>
> Sentí masculina urgencia
> y femenina ternura
> y fecundé con violencia
> y concebí con ternura (*Poemas*, p. 53)

In "Panadero" ("Baker," 1947), he uses the simple, humble image of bread to express the anguish of the poet who is able to create and bring happiness to others through his art, but is unable to achieve self-satisfaction:

> This bread I composed in life
> has never brought joy to me
> . . . .
> And today I die like a baker
> by the hot oven and the fire.
>
> Este pan que he compuesto en la vida
> nunca a mí me ha traído alegría.
> . . . .
> Y hoy me muero como un panadero
> junto al horno caliente y al fuego. (*Poemas*, p. 56)

"Poesía pura" ("Pure Poetry," 1962) can be seen as an "ars poetica." It is Arévalo's clearest statement in verse of the purposes, the limits, and the meaning of art. He rejects as artificial the concept that poetry is a superior, hermetic art available only to an initiated elite. Instead, he favors a simple poetry that makes no distinctions between poetic and nonpoetic topics and vocabulary. At the same time, he opposes the idea that poetry can be composed only with pure concepts, devoid of life and poetic form. Poetry, Don Rafael says, is the same for everyone and everything, whether it is found in gems, clay, procelain, or pottery; it is everywhere and nowhere at all:

for all it is the same, the gem, and the clay,
the Secres porcelain, and the lowly pot,
since it is everywhere and nowhere

para todos igual, la gema, el barro,
la vajilla de Sévres o el cacharro,
pues está en todas partes y en ninguna (*Poemas*, p. 60)

Arévalo's highest tribute to poetry appears in the poem "Fin" ("End," 1947). This sonnet expresses clearly how much he has enjoyed writing and how grateful he is for the gift of poetic creativity with which he has been blessed. He sings of an artist who has spent long years creating new worlds and "making dawn bloom in other lands" and who now sees death approaching. Old age has taken away his vigor, but he gathers his last strength to move to his desk, where he dies in the act of creation, falling forward on his last sonnet (*Poemas*, p. 58).

III *Life*

Arévalo Martínez has collected in this section of *Poemas* his reflections on life and living. He shows a surprisingly positive attitude, for although he realizes how limited the possibilities are for the human race, he gives himself up entirely to life, doing what needs to be done, without regrets. His eyes are not closed to the problems and the limitations of man, but he does not give up hope.

The earliest poems gathered in this section date from 1914. There is nothing exceptional in their language or concepts; they all use rather stilted images and ideas. For example, in "Títeres" ("Puppets"), he pictures life as a puppet show. He thinks that men are manipulated by nature, who by pulling threads makes them run after love, honor, and glory. This chase, however, is to no avail, because life is only a "transitory farce" (*Poemas*, p. 71). The poem "Ananké" ("Fate") reinforces this idea. Here Arévalo explains that man must make decisions constantly, but that these decisions are not really his own: although his future may be drastically changed, and his next step may bring happiness or agony, man is helpless, because he is not really in control of his life—everything happens according to the whims of fate (*Poemas*, p. 72). A strong sense of fatalism gives these two poems a feeling reminiscent of Romanticism and shows how little Arévalo had progressed at this time toward the development of a distinctive concept of life.

Don Rafael's mature poetry shows a definite change of attitude. In his later poems he seems to be at peace with himself and the world. He appears to have found his source of strength in living a natural and simple life. Many things around him still do not make sense, but he dedicates his efforts to those that do. He no longer worries unduly about people who pursue love, honor, and glory. Actually, he has decided that the most important thing in life is also the most basic—good health. In the poem "Vida" ("Life," 1947), he advises the reader that the most important characteristic one must look for in a wife is health. She must be a woman "with steel body and soul of diamond" ("de acero el cuerpo y de diamante el alma"), ready to carry on the serious business of living and passing on to her children her strength and her "capital of life" (*Poemas*, p. 68). Everything else is superfluous.

The realization of where the real values of life lie has given him security. He explains in the poem "Habla el salvaje" ("The Savage Speaks," 1947) how one may achieve this security. The poem begins with a rhetorical question about his strength: "Do you know the reason for the strength pent up in my soul?" ("¿Sabes por qué la fuerza que mi alma encierra?"), which he proceeds to answer in detail. Strength, he says, comes from nature, from living the way man was intended to live, in harmony with all creation, and with his bare feet firmly planted on the earth. Civilization, he believes, has made man sick; it has drained from him all his strength (*Poemas*, p. 67). This belief that progress is a disease appears again in the sonnet entitled "La Tierra" ("The Earth," 1962). Arévalo's strong respect and love for life make him reject any act of "civilization" that threatens to put an end to life on this planet. In this poem, nature, angered by man's atomic bomb, unleashes the fury of wind and water on the cities, erasing every sign of humanity from the land. Earth, restored to its primordial innocence, continues its trip through space:

> And it was again a silvered sphere,
> in the dawn of time,
> which innocently spun among the stars.

> Y fue de nuevo una plateada esfera,
> en la mañana de la edad primera,
> que rodó entre los astros inocentes. (*Poemas*, p. 68)

The fact that Don Rafael considers life one of the main themes of his poetry is especially interesting, since most poets have speculated more about death than about life. Death in this section of *Poemas* is simply a part of life, to be accepted with the same carefree attitude with which one accepts any other routine. In "Entrégate por entero" ("Give Yourself Wholly," 1947), the poet maintains that man should live a simple life, he should play hard, love hard, and work hard, living fully each minute of his existence. By the time death finally arrives, he will be ready to accept it willingly because, as the poet sees it, intense love of life automatically implies acceptance of death, a simple outgrowth of life (*Poemas*, p. 73).

The poem "Es necesario" ("It is Necessary," 1947) is built around the same notion: in order to live fully it is necessary to accept the fact of death ("es necesario el aceptar la muerte/para poder actuar sobre la vida"), but by the same token, in order to accept death it is necessary to know life ("para aceptar la muerte/es necesario conocer la vida"). Arévalo professes that his love for life is so complete that when his time comes he will be ready to enter without protest the mysterious door of oblivion (*Poemas*, p. 74).

IV *Home*

The home was ever the center of Don Rafael's life, the place where he found comfort and security, so it is not surprising that he devotes much of his poetry to this theme. Arévalo idealizes the home, seeing it as a refuge from life's daily cares, and as a warm, snug nest, isolated in time and space, where one finds the happy laughter of children and the contented, loving smile of the mother. Almost all the compositions gathered in this section are associated with his wife and children. "Dos hijos" ("Two Children") and "Criaturas gozosas" ("Happy Creatures"), written in 1915, refer tenderly to his young family. He portrays his two children, his wife, and himself as four helpless, innocent, little orphans:

> We are four shepherdless
> ermines.
> We are four orphaned
> children, Lord.

> Somos cuatro armiños
> que van sin pastor.
> Somos cuatro niños
> huérfanos. Señor. ("Two Children," *Poemas*, p. 132)

In "Happy Creatures" (1915), the mother, so pure, young, and beautiful ("tan pura, tan joven y tan bella"), surrounded by the laughter of her two children, becomes the center of the universe.

> . . . the fate of kings and nations
> weigh less on the scales of eternity
> than the pure, diaphanous happiness
> of these three innocent hearts.

> . . . el destino de reyes y naciones
> en balanzas eternas, pesan menos
> que la pura, la diáfana alegría
> de estos tres inocentes corazones. (*Poemas*, p. 142)

Arévalo Martínez confesses in "Sueño de ventura" ("Dream of Happiness," 1921) that his "dream" consists in being able to live in a fairytale sort of little town; a town hugged by mountains, with clear skies and a river near by. Here he would bring up his sons and daughters in rustic simplicity, so that they would grow to honor him and his wife in their old age (*Poemas*, pp. 125–26). He stresses in this poem once again the elements of innocence and simplicity developed from living in close contact with nature.

Arévalo Martínez's physical weakness and his lack of identification with the aggressive role assigned to man by society seem to determine his views on the family. His close relationship with his mother and his wife is apparent in his depiction of the role of woman. She is a dedicated homemaker, of strong character and happy disposition, who shields her family from the outside world by creating a relaxed, happy atmosphere around her. Man, on the other hand, has the role of the provider, a *puntal* ("prop"), as he describes himself in a poem by this title. Within the home, however, he is just as much in need of warmth and support as the children. The happy and relaxed atmosphere provided by the mother figure is essential to the husband's survival. In the poem "Hogar" ("Home," 1945), he admits that the wife occupies the supreme position; she makes the home: "A woman lights the hearth/and a man's heart warms to it" ("Una mujer enciende el fuego del hogar/y a él se calienta el corazón del hombre"). Arévalo speaks even more directly on this subject of man's debt to his wife in "Santa Evangelina" (1961), a poem he wrote for Eva on the occasion of their golden wedding anniversary:

I owe her all:
I owe her happiness
and the bread I eat each day
and the water I drink.
Without her, I would die.

Todo se lo debo:
le debo alegría
y el pan que por ella como cada día
y el agua que bebo.
Si ella me faltara yo me moriría. (*Poemas*, p. 145)

The sincere and moving acknowledgement of gratitude contained in this poem summarizes effectively Arévalo's feelings for his wife.

All the poetry in this section points to the fact that Don Rafael identifies home and woman to the extent that the first cannot exist without the second. They are the most important single item in his life, and without them life would hold little for him.

V *Religion*

Mysticism is a term that has been used often to describe the religious poetry of Arévalo Martínez.[11] One may or may not agree with this opinion, since agreeing is simply a matter of accepting a broad definition of the term mysticism; some critics have been in sharp disagreement.[12] It is undeniable, however, that religious themes do abound in his poetry and that some of the poems written in this vein show a high degree of artistic value and religious sensitivity.

Arévalo Martínez is a person of deep religious convictions. His beliefs were firmly instilled in him by the strict upbringing provided by the Catholic atmosphere of his home and of the "Colegio de Infantes." Though he lived through periods of doubt, which produced some serious crises in his adult life, eventually he was to return to the faith of his ancestors.[13] At times one finds in his poetry echoes of pantheism and even agnosticism, but the general tone is one of unwavering belief in God and the teachings of the Roman Catholic Church.

The dominant factor at the root of Arévalo's inspiration seems to be fear, a haunting apprehension that his sins will bring about his eternal damnation. Hounded by this doubt, he is moved to express unwavering faith in the infinite mercy of God. It is almost as if he expected his poems to act as some sort of charm, to exorcise evil and to reassure

God of his devotion. "Oración" ("Prayer," 1914) is one of the poems in which Arévalo speaks plainly about his fear. He openly admits that he is afraid; though he is not exactly sure of the reasons for being frightened, he realizes that he is guilty, and he knows of God's wrath. Don Rafael even admits that fear of being punished is what moves him to repent: "Forgive me, Lord; I have not loved you, but I have feared you" ("Señor, perdón; no te he amado, pero te he temido"). He hopes that his confession of his sins will move God to justice and forgiveness. There are many other poems, especially those written around 1914, that make reference to the poet's sins and to the need for God's forgiveness. Many of these poems do not openly refer to fear, although it is not difficult to sense that it is nonetheless present. Arévalo considers sin part of human nature; it is the animal side of man, always ready to do battle with the spirit. In "Malas bestias" (1914) he depicts men as "evil beasts," who seem to walk on all fours, because they do not deserve to walk on two feet.

> The divine spirit seems immured
> in the darkest recesses of a vicious beast
> because we carry it with us, cowering and wounded,
> and with our voices we still its voice.

> La siquis divina parece recluida
> en lo más oscuro de bestia feroz,
> porque la llevamos cobarde y herida
> y con nuestras voces callamos su voz. (*Poemas*, p. 169)

The poet begs God repeatedly to unburden him of his sins. In the sonnet "A Cristo" (1909), he asks Christ to allow him in His charity to rest on His bosom, the only place where he can fulfill his needs (*Poemas*, p. 180). He makes similar pleas in "Letanía" ("Litany," 1914), "Recibe mi oración" ("Receive my Prayer," 1914), "Jesús" (1914), and "Te suplicamos, ¡oh, Señor!" ("We Implore You, Oh, Lord!" 1947), to mention just a few of the many poems written to express his repentance and his anxiety for forgiveness.

Of the many sins of which he accuses himself, the worst seems to be his inability to believe fully in God. The constant doubts with which his reason assails him do not allow his faith to prevail. Even in his old age he continues to be haunted by his doubts, as attested by a poem—"Yo, el segundo Tomás" ("I, the Second Thomas")—that he wrote in 1955, at the age of seventy. In this composition, he begs Christ to allow him to place his hand on His wounds; like a "second

Thomas," he wants to make sure that he knows the truth (*Poemas*, p. 177).

Another prevalent motif in his religious poetry is the exaltation of God and His love. Among this group of poems, one of the most beautiful is "El girasol" ("The Sunflower," 1914). In it he utilizes the image of the sunflower to indicate his need to follow God, the source of all love. The humble flower teaches man a lesson of unselfishness by always being turned toward the source that sustains it, the sun: "Oh, with loving soul, like a sunflower/would that I could turn toward you, bright sun!" ("Oh, con alma amorosa, como un girasol, / quien pudiera estar vuelto hacia tí, claro sol!"). But the poet cannot turn toward God, because the deep roots of sin bind him to earth and prevent him from turning ("Mas con hondas raíces se extendió mi pecado/y no tengo la gracia de estar vuelto hacia Tí"—*Poemas*, p. 170). "Fuente escondida" ("Hidden Spring") plays with the language and vocabulary of the mystics to speak of the soul's "thirst" for God. Just as the thirsty person can recognize the hidden sources of water, the soul knows where to find divine love (*Poemas*, p. 162). "Qué importa" ("What Does it Matter," 1914) is a reflection on the poet's lack of importance: his life and problems are of no consequence; he thinks they are real, but they are only a passing illusion. The only real thing is God, who is life itself, and He will continue to live on. We do not exist: "And we are the ones who do not exist. / We who are only an illusion" ("Y nosotros somos los que no existimos. / Nosotros que somos sólo una ilusión"—*Poemas*, p. 181).

All the poems dealing with religious motifs show the great struggle going on in Arévalo Martínez's being. Though some of his compositions praise religious customs and events—"Nochebuena" ("Christmas Eve," 1942), "Navidad" ("Christmas," 1914), "Vía Crucis" ("The Way of the Cross," 1947), "Bienaventuranza"—"Beatitud," 1923)—in most cases he expresses deep feelings of anguish. His upbringing in the Judeo-Christian tradition of the Roman Catholic Church determines his attitude by predisposing him to think in terms of hell and damnation and to fear them. In his poems, God displays a dual personality: sometimes He is the Old Testament God of wrath and justice, while in some other instances He becomes the gentle and understanding God-Jesus, the humanized and loving divinity of the New Testament. But in either case, Arévalo Martínez's poetry shows his struggle to reconcile the religious concepts taught to him in his youth with the question his reason and modern thought forced him to ask—Does God exist? The poet answers in the affirmative, mostly because he needs to believe, but also because he is afraid not to believe.

VI *The Language of the Poet: Some Characteristics*

The critics of Arévalo's poetry are unanimous in praising the simplicity and straightforwardness of his poems. They almost make it sound as if his works were produced effortlessly and were completely devoid of rhetorical devices. Yet a close examination of his poetry reveals a complex technique carefully hidden in each deceivingly simple poem. The analysis of some of the devices favored by Arévalo Martínez in his mature works points to a most elaborate process of deornamentation. Instead of trying to impress the reader with contrived images, as he did in his youthful poems, he seems bent on hiding them to give the appearance of spontaneity.

His early works show a *preciosista* fondness for chromatic images. In addition to the colorful metaphors already mentioned in poems like "In the Jewelry Stores" or "The Poor Poet's Dream," there is an abundance of color in other works such as "Evil Eyes" ("chestnut eyes," "coffee diamonds," *Maya*, p. 13); "Blue Eyes" ("red carnations," "blue forget-me-nots," "sapphires," "blue butterfly," *Maya*, p. 65); "A Ring" ("eyes of blue sapphire," "black shawl," "pale golden hair," "blue veins," "marble skin," "ruby nails," *Maya*, pp. 66–67); "Silver Verses" ("silver fish," "white flower," "silver moon," "fertile gold").[14] In spite of this dazzling display, there is no particular originality in this visual imagery; the poet simply limits himself to the endless repetition of a series of clichés. The poems of his second phase, on the other hand, are almost completely devoid of color images. In his new poetry, Arévalo Martínez uses synesthesia in an understated manner. For example, "Ballad of Mature Love" builds its imagery around two deceivingly simple phrases that appear in the first line of the poem: "sweet night" and "sweet life." The adjective "sweet" is charged with a host of connotations suggested through its association with expressions taken from a common, familiar language ("sad soul," "silent love," "old comrade," "night aromas," "murmur of a lake"). "Sweetness" alludes, first of all, to the comfortable feeling created in his life by his wife: his "old comrade" gives him to drink a "youthful liquor" that contributes to the creation of a "sweet life." "Sweet night," on the other hand, carries a different, and yet similar, connotation; "night" is a symbol of old age and a premonition of death, but the modifying adjective "sweet," already charged with so much meaning, gives it a bittersweet feeling of resigned sadness, expressing concisely and effectively the poet's tranquil sorrow at growing old and seeing death approach. The masterfulness of Arévalo's art lies in his ability to convey complex feelings by using only the simplest of words and expressions.

The use of a great variety of parallelistic and correlative constructions is another device frequently and effectively used by Arévalo Martínez to create disarmingly simple poems. For example, the imagery in "Clean Clothes" is again built around two sensorial images taken from everyday speech: "I kissed her hand" (tactile) and "it smelled of soap" (olfactory):

I *kissed* her hand and it *smelled of soap:*
I *moved* mine *against* my heart.

I *kissed* her *small* and *delicate* hand
and my mouth was *perfumed.*

Clean girl, the one who dares approach you,
let him, like your hands *smell of new clothes.*

I *kissed* her *wavy tresses:*
why, they also *smelled of clean clothes!*

Le besé la mano y olía a jabón:
yo lleve la mía contra el corazón.

Le besé la mano breve y delicada
y la boca mía quedó perfumada.

Muchachita limpia, quien a ti se atreva,
que como tus manos huela a ropa nueva.

¡Besé sus cabellos de crencha ondulada:
si también olían a ropa lavada![15]

The parallel development of the sensorial images is evident only after careful analysis. The craftmanship is completely camouflaged by the simplicity of a language that flows as effortlessly as prose.

Arévalo frequently uses another form of parallelism to create a direct correspondence between several elements of a line or stanza. In some cases, the correlative use of words and concepts is further complicated by antithesis. In the poem "Portrait of a Woman,"

Arévalo says of the girl: "She is fat (A1), she is good (A2), she is happy (A3), and she is healthy (A4)." On the other hand, the protagonist-narrator is the exact opposite: "I love her because I am thin (B1), bad (B2), sad (B3) and useless (B4)" (*Atormentados*, p. 87). Perhaps the simplest forms of parallelism, and the most commonly used in Spanish popular poetry, are anaphora and alliteration. Both appear extensively in the poems of Arévalo Martínez. In "Baker" he effectively combines these devices in one short stanza: the anaphor emphasizes the constant, grinding work, while the alliteration "segado en la siega" recreates the soft sound of the sickle against the wheat and "muele el molino" reinforces the same concept and perception by referring to the milling of the grain:

> *With the grain* that the earth germinates,
> *with the grain* that is gathered in the harvest,
> *with the grain* the mill grinds,
> I composed my wheat bread.

> *Con el grano* que engendra la tierra,
> *con el grano* segado en la siega,
> *con el grano* que muele el molino,
> Yo compuse mis panes de trigo. (*Poemas*, p. 56; italics added)

The same parallelistic technique appears in "Luxury":

> Pity the girl,
> *the one with* the cheap perfume,
> *the one with* the pretty face,
> *the one with* the torn shoe

> ¡Lástima de muchachita,
> *la del* perfume barato,
> *la de la* cara bonita,
> *la del* raído zapato! (*Caminito*, p. 14; italics added)

The use of these artistic devices for the purpose of affecting casualness is typical of Arévalo Martínez's style. Also typical is the poet's tendency to choose the most simple, lowly images and vocabulary possible. Analysis of his themes and style proves that he is the creator of a rather low key poetry. By and large he deals with topics close to his daily life, expressing either his cares and anxieties or the joy of being alive. His themes did not change markedly over the years, but what did change was the mood and style. Don Rafael's first poems were patterned after those of the prevalent *preciosista* mode of the times. Most of them alluded to exotic places, luxurious elements, and decadent motifs, expressed in an artificially contrived, elegant language. All of these elements combined to produce some carefully wrought poems, but they lacked depth and originality and could not, therefore, satisfy Arévalo's longing for sincerity and commitment. His personal views on life and art developed according to those prevalent in his time. As the century progressed, the world witnessed serious disorders. Men came face to face with many problems of a social nature. Writers were forced to abandon their ivory towers and to confront the realities of life.

Arévalo's contribution to the new social consciousness in Spanish American poetry is a modest one. He is important only to the extent that he added his voice to the many others who tried to find new commitments and new avenues of expression. He chose a path of simplicity and sincerity that helped to bring poetry down from the lofty heights where the Romantics and early Modernists had left it. This change paved the way for poets who, like César Vallejo (Peru, 1892–1938) or Pablo Neruda (Chile, 1904–1973), would orient their poetry toward concern for man as a social being.

CHAPTER 3

The Early Psychological Novels

I *An Overall Glance at the Spanish American Novel*

THE novel is a relative newcomer to Spanish American literature. While the other genres, especially poetry, began to flourish and gain popularity immediately following the conquest, the novel, due to a variety of political, social, and historical reasons, did not make its first appearance until 1816.[1] In this year, the Mexican journalist José Joaquín Fernández de Lizardi (1776–1826) published the first Spanish American novel, a picaresque work entitled *El Periquillo Sarniento (The Itching Parrot)*. From this date on, novels were published in great numbers, but unfortunately, the quality of the works does not match their quantity. Early efforts to create a distinctive narrative produced meager results. As late as 1933, the distinguished Peruvian critic Luis Alberto Sánchez noted, in what was to become a very controversial book, *América: novela sin novelistas (America: Novel without Novelists)*, that in spite of the impressive number of novels written during the preceding one hundred years, Spanish America still could not boast a homogeneous group of novelists united by a distinctive style and a common philosophy of life.[2] He believed that the novelistic materials present on the Continent were powerful enough to overwhelm the authors, who by and large limited themselves to the objective reproduction of reality, with little attention to fantasy and imagination.

The novel was, however, undergoing slow but dramatic changes that would soon make it a dominant force in Spanish American letters. By 1939, the Chilean critic Arturo Torres Ríoseco could identify an impressive number of novelists who shared the characteristics Luis Alberto Sánchez had found lacking just a few years earlier.[3] Another Chilean critic, Fernando Alegría, believed that the task of creating this cohesive body of novels fell to the Regionalist and Modernist writers, who were the first to really discover Spanish

America's reality and to express it with new force and vitality. This was accomplished by a change of perspective, which turned the narrative away from the objective sociorealistic approach used by the late nineteenth and early twentieth century writers toward the presentation of a new and more subjective vision of reality, a vision that was a product of inner reality.[4]

The writers of the first quarter of the twentieth century found themselves caught in a dilemma. Their roots still bound them to traditional Spanish Realism and moral commitment, while the new literary currents pushed them toward subjectivism, with emphasis on idealism and aestheticism. The two currents coexisted for a number of years, while the writers tried to determine their true allegiance. Some eventually found an answer in an escape to European culture, but others continued to pursue the development of autochthonous themes and the creation of new ways of expressing their immediate reality. This latter group of writers would finally make the most original contribution to the development of Spanish American prose fiction. The indigenous mode of expression they developed exhibited a new sensibility. It utilized the themes made popular by Realism, but it expressed them in the careful style inherited from Modernism. The door was then open for the triumph, in the second half of the twentieth century, of a different type of work. The new novel that finally evolved uses native subject matter but does not limit itself to the Spanish American themes that were the main concern during the preceding period of self-analysis and definition. Instead, it has rejoined the currents of European thought as an equal, showing deep concern for aesthetic and philosophical principles.

II *Arévalo Martínez's Place in Spanish American Fiction*

The Modernist belief in artistic freedom allowed each writer to experiment at will. The result was a multifaceted narrative that reflected the personality and the individual goals of each artist. The only thing these writers had in common was the cult of form and beauty, the conscious desire to develop a language capable of reflecting the new sensibility. For the most part, they created artistic novels that allowed them to evade what they considered to be their drab surroundings. Through their works, they escaped to exotic lands or to an interior ivory tower from whose splendid isolation they could examine the inner recesses of their souls. Each writer was unique; each contributed different but basic and irreplaceable elements to the development of the novel. Together they created a veritable storehouse of dynamic artistic possibilities that were to be exploited by succeeding generations of novelists.

Rafael Arévalo Martínez has the distinction of being a forerunner of the new fictional trends. He is the one who first succeeded in erasing the barriers between reality and fantasy, thus becoming, among many other things, a precursor of Magic Realism.[5] According to Kessel Schwartz, this particular trait of his works makes him a distant reflection of many of today's top novelists, a most important link in the development of the genre.[6] Arévalo's contributions to the field of prose fiction are so varied and important that Kessel Schwartz considers him the single most influential author in clearing the way for the new novel:

He might be classified as a criollista, as a social novelist, as a surrealist, and, as he most often is, as a modernist; but his leaven of mystery and apocalyptic and monstrous vision of man, and his treatment of nonhuman souls in human bodies are the stuff of magic realism. His characters are neither heroes nor anti-heroes and seem to be "agonists" of reality not subject to stereotypes. Arévalo inherited much from Poe, Lautréamont, and Nerval, but in spite of these remote ancestors the beginning of the new novel belongs to him.[7]

The value of Arévalo Martínez's narrative is undeniable, but placing him categorically within one school or movement is practically impossible; his works show, and sometimes suffer from, the endless experimentation in which all Modernist writers engaged in their continuous search for beauty and perfection. The novel is perhaps the field where Arévalo's sometimes abrupt changes of direction can be most easily observed. Thus in his early novels, he emphasized the psychological analysis of the protagonist, while later works show a high degree of social concern: they are comments on dictatorship, anti-imperialism, and the creation of utopian worlds.

III Una vida

Seymour Menton believes that *Una vida* (*A Life*, 1914) is important because it represents the first effort by a Guatemalan author to bare his soul.[8] Arévalo Martínez is known as a consummate portrayer of character, but his keen insight was developed by searching into the deepest recesses of his own soul. Don Rafael's nearsightedness circumscribed his world to a narrow radius, and within the limited range of his vision, there were not very many things worth exploring.

The only exceptions were the people with whom he came into contact. They stood out against the hazy background of his myopic world and thus became the prime object of his concern; he observed and analyzed them until, eventually, he became an accomplished judge of human character and one of the best delineators of psychological portraits.

The lonely years of his sickly childhood and adolescence taught him to rely on his own resources: reading and daydreaming were his most important sources of entertainment. As he grew older he became fascinated by his own psyche: he concentrated on his emotions and on his reactions to the world around him. The analysis of his hypersensitive personality became a far more important source of inspiration than the observation of external reality or the creation of an imaginary world.

In *A Life,* a very short autobiographical novel—forty-six small pages—Arévalo Martínez presents his early life. The story begins with his first day at school, at age five, and ends with his graduation from the "Colegio de Infantes" some thirteen years later. Outwardly not much happens to the protagonist during these years. Spiritually, however, there is a turmoil of emotions, which the author analyzes to show the makeup of a neurasthenic personality.

Arévalo Martínez divides the book into two parts. The narrator begins by concentrating on a nostalgic impression of his first day at school and by describing his sadness at being separated from his mother. Next, he tells about the year he spent at the kindergarten in which he had his first schooling under the watchful eyes of the owner, a middle-aged woman he called *la señorita.* The girls in the group of twenty children had the opportunity to begin embroidery, a skill that belonged exclusively to the feminine world. This subject, however, fascinated the little boy; it was difficult for him to hide his envy and his admiration when he saw the beautiful designs, the green butterflies, and the red trees that emerged from his sister's chubby hands. Although they were clumsily stitched, his child's eyes saw them as the creation of an enchanted and magic world of color.[9]

Many of his youthful actions had future repercussions. He explains, for example, his joy, shared by his family and his teacher, at having learned to read in two weeks. He was showered with praises and congratulations, as well as with a prize consisting of each denomination of silver coin then used in Guatemala. In retrospect, however, Arévalo judges this accomplishment in a different light. It was, he said, one more sign of his precociousness, a trait that quickly helped him surpass the knowledge of all the boys in his class. As a result, he was moved to the girls' circle, an action that brought bitter emotional consequences. The envious boys avenged themselves by calling him, among other sarcastic epithets, "Blessed among women" ("Bendito entre las mujeres"). Thus, he says, began a persecution that would end only with his death (*Vida*, p. 12).

His reading ability also proved to be a disadvantage because it led his mother to nurture false hopes for a great future. As Arévalo saw it, precocity was the gift of those born old in spirit. These unfortunate persons, never having been children, do not have a chance to be men. This is the reason why he, like a eunuch, would go from infancy to old age, without having attained virility (*Vida*, pp. 13–14). This statement clearly points out how insecure of his manhood he was. His attraction for what society disdainfully considers feminine activities, coupled with his physical weakness, had created in him a deep-rooted sense of sexual inadequacy.

Arévalo's fascination with reading, however, shaped his whole life. He describes his affair with books in terms of drug addiction. He considers it a vice, a drug necessary to sedate his raw emotions. The only way he could survive the harsh world around him was by becoming oblivious to reality through the opium of fantasy. He admits that fiction was as necessary to him as alcohol to an alcoholic. As a result of all his reading, he developed a second, false and deformed, extrahuman nature (*Vida*, pp. 16–17), a "literary personality" that would handicap him for many years.

The second part of *A Life* narrates his misery at the "Colegio de Infantes." His attitude had not changed at all, and he continued to be plagued by his still undiagnosed nearsightedness, which gave him the shyness and lack of security typical of a person who could not even recognize his sister at a distance of twenty paces. His new and now older classmates tormented him mercilessly, and he reacted to them with such a mixture of shyness and terror that it simply provoked them to make him the brunt of their cruel pranks. Each incident pushed the author-narrator further into a world of fantasy. To escape, he read voraciously, almost to the point of abandoning his studies completely. Through his reading, he became acquainted with Alphonse Daudet's *The Little Thing,* and he marveled at the way the French writer had been able to portray his own sensibility while describing himself (*Vida*, p. 33).[10]

The boy reacted to his classmates' actions with a strange mixture of fear and boastfulness—he called it pain and daydream. The terror of confronting them would make him resist going to school every morning: he unsuccessfully invented imaginary illnesses, cried, and begged his mother for one day of reprieve. But at other times, inspired by the heroic deeds of the Three Musketeers, he would conquer his chronic fear and attack his tormentors, only to end up in retreat. Aware of his acute cowardice, he tortured himself with endless self-accusations (*Vida*, p. 35).

As life at school settles into a routine, the narrator omits the monotony of the intervening years and skips to the only other important event of his school career—his graduation. He explains that for years he had passed his courses thanks to teachers' pity and to his last minute efforts. Then, suddenly, two years before graduation, he became aware of his responsibilities. Love for his mother pushed him to make her happy by trying to graduate with honors. He did: gathering all his strength, he studied hard enough to win ten silver medals, which quickly became ten empty symbols, useless in the struggle for life. Ironically, the work he had done was too strenuous for his weak constitution, and he found himself in a sick bed. Arévalo finishes the book with this bitter statement: at eighteen years of age, he was declared by his doctor incapable of doing anything; and life declared him incapable of living. His existence proved that he was nothing, that he did nothing. He could be defined by three clarifying words: "a decadent poet," he was just one more decadent Spanish American poet (*Vida*, p. 46).

In *A Life*, Arévalo Martínez is obviously the protagonist. Many of the details correspond to his character and personal life. However, he attempts to cover up, protecting his own identity by changing the most obvious external aspects of his life. Thus, in the novel, he eliminates his father and describes himself as the oldest child of a poor, sickly widow; instead of a brother and several sisters, his fictional persona has only a sister, Adela. These changes also have an artistic purpose, since they create a sentimental aura around the protagonist. The reader is expected to react with immediate sympathy toward the poor little fatherless child whose life is surrounded by so much melodramatic tragedy. He is marked by fate from the beginning and through no fault of his own. He is the *man* of the family, the only hope his widowed mother and sister have for a better future. But he is a sick child with a morbid personality. Unable to fulfill the masculine role society expects of him, he retires into a world of fantasy and acquires a lopsided education that does not prepare him to survive in the real world.

IV   Manuel Aldano

Manuel Aldano (1922), subtitled *A Struggle for Life*, forms a novelistic unit with *A Life*. Arévalo Martínez picks up the narrative thread exactly where his first novel left it and recounts what happened to the protagonist after his graduation. All his fears about the future are realized in this novel. In *A Life*, he was a child, and although he had been exposed to the cruelties of other children, he did not have to worry about serious responsibilities. In *Manuel Aldano*, on the other hand, he enters the world of grownups and finds himself as vulnerable and unqualified to cope with its expectancies as he had been ill-prepared to confront his classmates.

Arévalo Martínez concentrates once again on psychological analysis rather than action. There is, however, a thin plot that tells of the protagonist's painful progression through a series of jobs— salesman, helper of a Jewish banker, and finally, clerk in the Banco Agrícola.

Manuel Aldano has a prologue in which Arévalo asks for the reader's indulgence. He says that although he is aware of the novel's lack of relevance, he is publishing it as an encouragement to the weak and sick in society; he wants to teach them trust, resignation, and hope. The prologue sets the mood for the series of misfortunes and little crises that occur to the protagonist as he sets out to make a place for himself and his family in society.

Arévalo concentrates on describing Aldano's feelings of inadequacy and shame as he fails to make his life meaningful. His constant failures create, of course, a vicious circle; since his hypersensitivity makes a crisis of major proportions out of every small happening, he feels persecuted and mistreated and takes refuge at home, systematically quitting his jobs as pressure and responsibility begin to mount. Once jobless, he goes into a period of remorse that sends him to bed, physically ill from his psychological problems. Thus, low self-esteem contributes to his failure, and each failure further complicates the problem by feeding his sense of inadequacy.

The feeling of uselessness is the most obvious trait and the most often analyzed characteristic of the protagonist. He is acutely ashamed of it. When he finally lands an unpaying position as apprentice at the *El Aguila* shop, he is overwhelmed by happiness, but once at the store, he does not know what to do with himself. When he tries to be helpful, the other employees ignore him or are irritated by him. The owner finally asks him to do something: first he must sprinkle the floor with water and then sweep it. He has been assigned the lowest of all jobs available, and the owner, knowing of the young man's pride in his recently awarded high school diploma, adds insult to injury by addressing him as *bachiller*. [11]

This episode is a perfect example of the way he magnifies the most unimportant details. Aldano takes the watering can and goes to fill it up across the street. His feelings at this moment overwhelm him. He has difficulty expressing and analyzing them: he is ashamed of being seen doing such a menial job; he feels all the passers-by are staring at him. At the same time, he is proud of having a job. He has been taught that any kind of job is honorable, since it proves he is capable of doing something useful. The mixed feelings produce a half-ashamed, half-pained reaction in the protagonist and at the same time a vague sense of anguish. When he returns to the store, after what his abnormal sensitivity pictures as a great adventure, he finds himself faced with an insurmountable problem: his almost blind eyes do not even allow him to see clearly the floor he must clean. He breaks out in a cold sweat; drops the watering can, which shatters with a loud explosion; and ruins several pieces of merchandise. The realization that he is not even capable of sweeping the floor makes him decide that he is even in worse condition than a cripple, since outwardly he looks normal.

The pathos created by this small incident makes the protagonist comment on the meaning of existence as he wonders why his strength never measures up to his high aspirations of absolute perfection (*Aldano*, pp. 15–16). Aldano is aware of his tendency to exaggerate. He says at one point that his sickly sensibility has hurt him in his struggle for life by forcing him to make a mountain out of each molehill. As one who has been stripped of skin in body and soul, he responds to the slightest touch. No callus has ever developed to protect his sensitive soul (*Aldano*, p. 53). It is true that as the novel progresses, he never gets over his extreme sensitivity, but he does start accepting his ineptitude. At some point he realizes that the fact that he knows the limits of his physical capabilities gives him the advantage of being able to adapt himself to circumstances and to lower his expectations. The problem is that his soul will never learn to adapt (*Aldano*, p. 99).

The employment he finally found at the Banco Agrícola was the best he had held in three years of hard luck. He worked indefatigably to become proficient. Much to the irritation of the cleaning crew, he arrived at the bank three hours before opening time to practice and learn. He was so proud of his accomplishments that he even became reconciled to his nearsightedness because it allowed him to do his close range work without problems. In spite of his inner contentment, he was still physically weak. The excesses to which he subjected himself to keep up with the job eventually took their toll. He became so exhausted that he could no longer concentrate on anything other than the thought of resting. At one point it took him three hours to do a simple mathematical calculation; his fingers and his brain were numb. One day he arrived at work and sat at his desk, fixedly watching a spider make its web. There was nothing in his mind except pain, a vague feeling of pain. After what seemed like an eternity, he became conscious of his surroundings and was overwhelmed by such violent feelings of revulsion for the bank and all it meant that he walked away from his job, never to return (*Aldano*, pp. 130–31). The spider is the perfect symbol for Arévalo's relationship with the external world. He continuously wove a web to connect himself to society; then, finding himself trapped in his own web, he would destroy it.

Manuel Aldano, confused and hurt once more, took refuge at home. He slept for three days; after awakening, he remained in bed, resting and meditating, for one month. As strength returned to his body, so did the feelings of failure and his rebelliousness against it. He finally decided to seek contact with the outside world and began taking long walks around the city. As he observed the miserable conditions in which his compatriots lived, his social consciousness was aroused. There occurred to him a parallelism that allowed the introduction of a social theme into the novel: Aldano linked the illness of his body to the disintegration of Guatemala. The tropical heat and diseases that fed on Guatemala had reduced her to the condition of an invalid, just as the neurasthenia that fed on his soul had caused his downfall. They both needed a doctor.

The introduction of social criticism breaks the thematic unity of the novel. It does show, however, that Arévalo Martínez, in spite of his narcissistic tendencies, was not completely unaware of social problems. He, like Rodó, Darío, and many other Modernists, had begun to take notice of Spanish America's plight and would become more and more outspoken and critical as time went on. In *Manuel Aldano*, Arévalo had some harsh words for the lack of ambition in the majority of the "Indo-Latin" population: they allowed themselves to be manipulated by the many foreign companies that bled Guatemala. The Anglo-Saxon exploiters are compared to brooms: they come in,

sweep up the profits, and return home. Arévalo is proud of his
Spanish background, and he defends the rich, humanistic, Latin
tradition of which he, like most Modernists, feels a part:

Now also, the vivacious Latins, thoughtful and sentimental, intelligent and
languid, given to fostering all forms of the arts, very civilized, according to a
certain concept of civilization, were being overrun by the blue-eyed,
steel-armed barbarians from the North. The enslaving North was very near:
its name was Yankeeland. The conquering North was very near: the ocean
having been eliminated by Fulton or Curtis, its name was Germany....

También ahora, sobre el vivaz latino, expeculativo y sentimental, inteligente
y lánguido, dado al cultivo de todas las artes, muy civilizado, en cierto
concepto de la civilización, bajaban los bárbaros del Norte, de pupilas
celestes y brazos de acero. Muy próximo estaba el Norte avasallador: se
llamaba Yanquilandia. Muy cerca estaba el Norte avasallador: suprimido el
océano por Fulton o por Curtis, se llamaba Alemania.... (Aldano, pp.
140–41)

He warns Latin America to take notice and to counter the maneuvers
of Yankee imperialism before it is too late.

   Manuel Aldano makes it evident that at this point in his life,
Arévalo Martínez had come to realize that he was not the center of the
universe. This personal discovery gave a new direction to his
narrative. Except for Las noches en el Palacio de la Nunciatura
(Nights at the Palace of the Nunciature), political and social themes
predominated in all the novels he wrote after Manuel Aldano. One
can also observe in this novel the first manifestations of other themes
and techniques that have been identified with Arévalo Martínez's
works. Thus, along with the innumerable personal references to his
character and emotions, he also shows a keen sensitivity to other
people's idiosyncrasies. He very specifically associates human and
animal traits, a technique fully exploited in his psycho-zoological
stories. For example, after describing the nephew of a Catalonian
shopkeeper in great detail, Arévalo ends in a manner common to his
psychological portraiture:

And by a strange physical law, which gives to all men more or less the
appearance and even the characteristics of an animal and which seems to be
the mark with which the Creator stamped the unity of all created things, that
man looked exactly like a bird; or rather like a baby bird. His glasses added to
this effect. There are birds with such round eyes that they appear to wear
glasses.... He seemed a half-blind little bird; a little bird who appeared to

be defenseless, but whom we see attacking other birds with his beak; with his weak beak and small claws he fought for his grain, his insect, and his mate with other winged rivals; he was a little bird of a slightly malevolent species, like a sparrow, so cruel with his fellow birds. But, after all is said, he was a bird who inspired trust.

Y por una extraña ley física, que da a todos los hombres más o menos el aspecto y hasta las características de un animal y parece ser la firma con que el Creador selló la unidad de todo lo creado, aquel hombre tenía todo el aspecto de un pájaro; o más bien, el de un pichón de pájaro. Contribuían a ello hasta sus lentes. Hay aves de ojos redondos que parecen tener lentes.... Semejaba un pajarillo semiciego; un pajarillo al parecer inerme y al que vemos, sin embargo, atacar a picotazos a sus congéneres; con el piquillo débil y las menudas garras, disputar el grano, el insecto o la hembra a los rivales alados; un pajarillo de una especie un poco malévola, como los gorriones, tan crueles con sus semejantes. Pero, al fin de todo, un pajarillo que inspiraba confianza. (*Aldano*, p. 70)

Another theme that emerges in this novel is self-criticism, not only of his weaknesses and defects, but even more importantly, of his literary works and his religious beliefs. Aldano's acute neurosis leads him to seek the advice of Dr. Esquerdo. His many conversations with the doctor are, for artistic purposes, reduced to only one. The narrator gives the highlights of what turns out to be almost a soliloquy in which Aldano begins to pose himself questions of great transcendental value. After discussing his illness, they move on to more significant matters such as the emotions, art, ethics, and science versus religion.

Because the doctor has developed a deep affection for his patient, he quite frankly discusses with him the nature of his illness. Dr. Esquerdo believes Aldano to be an acute example of neurasthenia, destined to end up in a mental asylum. He tells his young patient that his metaphysical anguish has a physical cause: it is a product of his sick nerves. The problem is, he adds, that his degenerating system does not allow him to realize that he will never be able to grasp the absolute. Aldano answers that it is easy enough for the doctor to dismiss his thirst for the absolute as the product of mental illness. If Esquerdo were right, he asks, what would be the difference between a saint and a madman, between a hero and an insane person? The doctor does not answer this question, saying that Aldano's thoughts are too cloudy to reason out anything. In order to prove this last point, the doctor argues that Aldano, because of his mental illness, is incapable of writing anything that does not deal with himself. Therefore, his works show strong emotions and a deplorable state of mind. In the ensuing discussion, Aldano's defense of passion makes the doctor take the side of science, and he is greatly amazed when Aldano confesses that he has never understood the incompatibility some people see between science and religion. His quest for the absolute, he says, has now taken him back to the simple faith of his ancestors, and he is convinced that the same ethics underlie every belief; religious differences are a matter of terminology (*Aldano*, pp. 109–16). The metaphysical discussion ends here, but Arévalo Martínez will continue to treat this subject in a number of fictional works, as well as in his essay *Concepción del Cosmos* (*Concept of the Universe*, 1954).

A Life and *Manuel Aldano* are characterized by a direct, amiable style. The author's Modernism is evident in the morbid sensibility of the protagonist, rather than in any *preciosista* experimentation with language.[12] The narrator presents the few facts necessary to understand his life chronologically and then quickly dispenses with them in order to concentrate on a description of every emotion and mood experienced by his sensitive psyche.

In these novels, Arévalo Martínez concentrates on the description of his own emotions because he believes every novelist should deal with the subject he knows best. In a paper he prepared for a Guatemalan radio program in 1965, he discusses the characteristics of the genre. He explains that the novel is the highest literary form of expression and that its value depends on its exactness, its language, and the interest generated by the particular scene described. He assigns the preeminent place among the different types of novels to those which copy life objectively and with precision. He believes this is what he has done in his first two novels:

When he [an author] writes his autobiography in the first person or when he tells his experiences, he is objective, because he unfolds his own self, living again. My novels *Una vida* and *Manuel Aldano* offer these traits. The *reader-subject* has in front of him a character who, while retelling his childhood and his youth, becomes an *object of perception,* while he expresses his lyrical subjectivity. This happens because an author who writes autobiographically is the equivalent, in the most objective genre of all, the theater, of one lonesome character involved in a long monologue.

Cuando escribe en primera persona su autobiografía, o relata sus experiencias, es objetivo, pues desdobla su propio yo, viviendo de nuevo. Mis novelas

Una vida y *Manuel Aldano* ofrecen estos caracteres. El *sujeto lector* tiene ante sí, en ellas, a un personaje que, al referirle su infancia y su juventud, mientras más expresa la subjetividad propia de un poeta lírico, más le caracteriza un buen *objeto de percepción*. Porque un autor que escribe autobiográficamente equivale, en la mayor de las objetividades, la del teatro, a un personaje único, en un largo monólogo.[13]

Arévalo Martínez believes that an author, in addition to being objective, must also be free to choose his style and subject matter and must have the innate originality to create his own fictional world, precepts that he observed in the writing of his first two novels. He chose themes that had not before been treated in Spanish American literature, and he had the ability to handle them effectively and the originality to innovate stylistically by employing a simple, unaffected language, far removed from the *preciosista* style of the early Modernists, the melodramatic, sentimental manner of the late Romantics, and the crude technique of the Naturalists. His success accelerated the development in Spanish American literature of a more personal, sincere approach to the narrative genre.

V   Las noches en el Palacio de la Nunciatura

Las noches en el Palacio de la Nunciatura y Sentas (Nights at the Palace of the Nunciature and Sentas) is a volume published in 1927 containing two separate works.[14] The first, a novel, gives its title to the book; the second, *Sentas*, is, according to Kessel Schwartz,[15] Arévalo's first novelette, a minor love story written in 1910.[16] From the point of view of understanding the development of Arévalo Martínez's art and personality, *The Nights at the Palace of the Nunciature* is by far the more interesting of the two. The narrator is Manuel Aldano once again, but this time the tale does not concentrate on the analysis of his exacerbated emotions; instead, it centers on his reactions to the other two main characters, who serve as catalysts for Aldano's ideas. By using this technique the author can explore two rather sensitive topics—the occult and homosexuality —without becoming personally involved. He acts as a detached observer reporting on how the spirits directly affect another's life.

Arévalo Martínez's fascination with spiritualism developed from several sources. He must have become acquainted with this subject through books, for the occult was a fairly common theme in nineteenth century literature. It became an important source of inspiration following the Age of Reason and the abolition of official religion by the French Revolution, an action that obviously created a spiritual void. Anna Balakian comments that the metaphysical thirst of the times was satisfied by the theories of Swedenborg,[17] who became "the patron saint of too many ideologies, philosophies, and literary trends."[18] Swedenborgian thought was assimilated by the Symbolists and eventually by the Modernists. It is easily identified in many works of Arévalo Martínez.

Don Rafael must have also encountered the occult in the Guatemalan milieu. By the very fact that he lived in Central America, he had to be acquainted with two other important sources of spiritualist thought. One is the Roman Catholic Church's belief in the world of the spirits. Although the church forbids seances and rejects the idea that man can willfully interfere with the spirits, it certainly admits that they do exist: God, the saints, and the angels, as well as Satan and the devils, are spirits who do intervene in the lives of men whenever it fits God's (or the Devil's) purposes. In Guatemala this belief is reinforced by the remnants of the animistic Mayan religion, still practiced by thousands of Indians in Central America. Actually, through the superimposition of one religion on the other, many of the rites and beliefs of these two religions have become fused into one in the popular mind. This syncretism has created a special brand of Catholicism with curious practices and rituals for the cult of the dead.

Aside from these likely literary and social influences, Arévalo Martínez had a closer personal contact with the occult. He admits that although his father was a very devout Catholic, his mother believed in spiritualism. When he was eighteen years old, his mother's sister introduced him to the Ouija and thus to the world of the spirits. His curiosity was so aroused by the spiritualist experiences that followed that he studied innumerable religions and philosophies.[19] His curiosity was never satisfied, but the occult continued to intrigue him for the rest of his life.

The occult appears to be a source of fascination for many human beings. In his book *The Way Down and Out*, John Senior defends the concept of the occult as a kind of *philosophia perennis* that is the unifying force underlying all rituals and theologies. He thinks that "occultism" is the family resemblance that exists among all separate religions.[20] The resemblance is due to the fact that there are at least three basic beliefs shared by all primitive people: "(1) the universe is animate; (2) there is an animating 'force'; (3) this force can be controlled through sympathy and contagion in various kinds of rituals and discipline." Professor Senior further explains that these beliefs, although contained in all primitive religions, are not necessarily primitive beliefs: "They are held by people who are neither charlatans nor fools in our own time and are the basis of the 'occult' world view in all times and places."[21] Arévalo's discussion of the occult in *The Nights at the Palace of the Nunciature* shows a general accord with the theories of Senior.[22]

In this novel the reader meets a Manuel Aldano whose life and character have changed a great deal. He is no longer the insecure, timid young man struggling to make a place for himself in society. Now he is a mature individual, married to Andrea, a young girl he proudly describes as healthy in soul and body, illiterate, and with her own two feet firmly planted on the ground. She is a happy, sweet, and prolific woman, who has given her husband many children and will give him many more still. They live in a cozy nest, easily identified with the one Arévalo Martínez lovingly refers to in his poetry. He is content, and his morbid nature has mellowed somewhat due to his wife's optimistic nature. Their contrasting characters produce a happy union that assures Aldano's triumph in the struggle for life. He has become a worthy member of society, one who can boast of a steady job that provides a modestly adequate living for his wife and children. Measured by society's rules, he is now a respectable pater familias.

In the first part of the novel, the peaceful family life is unexpectedly interrupted by the visit of an unusual personage, José Meruenda. He simply knocks at the door one day and introduces himself. The fat and healthy-looking Meruenda produces two strong and contradictory impressions on Aldano:

the first sensation was one of youth, candor, and liveliness; the second threw a shadow of sin and grief over the first one; this second sensation was so embarrassing that sometimes Meruenda's angel face became grotesque to the point of being painful to the beholder. He was as fresh as a ripe tropical fruit, but grotesque like the low mentality of an obscene man. . . .

la primera de estas sensaciones era de juventud, de ingenuidad, de vida; la segunda tendía una sombra de pecado y de dolor sobre todo esto; y esta segunda sensación era a veces tan penosa que la cara de angelote de Meruenda se volvía grotesca hasta causar pena. Fresco como una fruta del trópico en plena madurez, grotesco como la baja mentalidad de un hombre obsceno. . . . [23]

Aldano's original impressions would be confirmed through his subsequent dealings with the strange character. In the first day of Meruenda's visit, however, Aldano was charmed by his innocent, childlike nature and, upon finding out that he had no money and no job, invited him to stay at his home for twenty days. Aldano stipulated that at the end of this period, Meruenda would leave willingly without having to be reminded that his time was up. Meruenda moved in with everyone's approval, but the situation did not remain stable very long. The family soon began to notice peculiar happenings that Arévalo narrates in a series of very entertaining anecdotes. For example, the day of Meruenda's arrival they discovered his extreme gluttony: not only did he eat enormous amounts of food, but he also consumed everybody's dessert, while the children watched tearfully. His fondness for food produces several of the hilarious incidents told by Arévalo Martínez as part of the delineation of Meruenda's base character. Next, in a crescendo effect, the author narrates a series of incriminating actions, each more damaging than the one before. Thus, the family discovers that Meruenda's deep religious convictions are nothing but a façade to impress the Aldanos; that the many presents he receives from an assortment of friends are actually a series of stolen objects; that Meruenda is wearing Andrea's silk stockings; and finally, after he has left the house, they learn that Meruenda is a homosexual and a child molester. The first part of the novel ends on the bitter note that he has given a "shameful sexual disease" to a friend's two young children.

All incidents in the first part of the novel deal with Meruenda's dubious life and character. Everything is logically and objectively presented. There is only one inexplicable event: late one night the Aldanos heard blood-curdling moans; they opened their bedroom door, and Meruenda, disfigured by fright, rushed in to hide at the foot of their bed. Aldano questioned him repeatedly and unsuccessfully until, finally, he seized him by the neck and forced him to go back to his room. After they entered and lighted a candle, he begged Aldano to remain until he was in bed and covered up to his eyes and allowed him to leave only after he had promised that the light would burn all night. The incident remained unexplained.

The mood and the style of the second part are quite different. In the opening paragraph, Aldano announces that the magnificent Mr. Aretal (the protagonist of "The Man Who Looked Like a Horse") has sent a telegram informing him that he is coming to Guatemala. Aldano is elated at the prospect of a reunion with a soul as restless as his own, and his anticipation is so intense that his wife, in jest, tells him that he could hardly be more excited if the most beautiful girl in the world were coming to see him (*Noches*, p. 39).

Aretal and Aldano reminisce about their past experiences in images that recall Arévalo's earlier works on Aretal. During the long talk that follows, Aretal mentions Meruenda and the mysterious spiritualist experiences they had shared in Mexico City. Aldano prods him, but his friend refuses to say more, although he promises to do so when there is plenty of sunlight around. Aretal later tells Aldano that Meruenda moved into his apartment at the Palace of the Nunciature in Mexico City and that strange things immediately began to happen: objects flew through the air, horrendous noises were heard, objects were thrown at people, people were pursued by objects, and so forth. Eventually, these phenomena became public knowledge, and the apartment was overrun by an assortment of newspapermen, theosophists, and spiritualists, creating such an impossible situation that Aretal was forced to move out.

The day following the retelling of the events, Aretal wondered aloud if Aldano thought that these odd experiences were the product of his association with drugs. Aldano assured him that he believed the answer to be far more simple: without elaborating, he said that everything could be explained by means of spiritualist practices.

At a subsequent meeting, Aretel tells Aldano of Meruenda's latest exploits in Mexico City. Meruenda had been introduced into Mexico's highest social circles by a rich widow with whom he was having a love affair. He had become so daring that he had published some of Aretal's poems under his own name and had impersonated the French ambassador at an official reception given in his honor by the Mexican president. Aldano was appalled at these new revelations and rather perplexed that Meruenda had carried out his pranks with impunity. Aretal answered ironically that the country could not afford a scandal because it had to protect its national pride and prestige from international ridicule. The second part of the novel ends with this comical narration of Meruenda's adventures.

The last section of *The Nights at the Palace of the Nunciature* is a metaphysical discussion on the occult and the nature of man's relationship with God and the universe. Arévalo Martínez handles this conversation in a manner reminiscent of that between the narrator and Dr. Esquerdo in *Manuel Aldano*. The two friends are enclosed in a windowless room; there Aretal throws his ideas at Aldano, almost as if he were his alter ego, involved in a long, anguished monologue.

Aldano the mystical poet and Aretal the *poète maudit* debate the question of life and death and its implications for humanity. Aretal proposes that there is only one central Being and that all things are His manifestations. Any sign of the spirit is the triumph of the Godlike nature of man over his material side. The exaltation produced by their conversation induces a mystical state during which they find themselves united with the cosmos. Both are one; all the universe is one. The difference among a tree, a dog, or a man is a matter of the degree of refined consciousness (spirit) that animates them.

As they begin to come out of their trance, the discussion turns to commiseration with man's situation. They compare humanity to Christ on the Cross. Man fights against his base instincts in order to share in the spiritual nature of God. Aretal and Aldano cry together, anguished by the realization that they are only men, ephemeral beings who identify with their miserable bodies. They see that man's nature is the epitome of contradiction—he is the lowest and the highest form of creation: he is limited by his human condition, but the spirit that animates him makes him aspire to wisdom and omniscience. Ironically, as man's consciousness rises he suffers the more, because such is the essence of being man—to be conscious is to suffer (*Noches*, p. 99).

Aldano finally rebuffs all of his friend's ideas with one simple Latin exclamation: "Credo licet absurdum" ("Although absurd to do so, I believe"—*Noches*, p. 99). He then runs home to kneel in front of Christ's image and to ask forgiveness for having allowed the words of Aretal to find an echo in his own conscience.

The general outline of Aldano's relationship with Meruenda and Aretal is autobiographical. Only minor details, essential to the effective artistic development of the novel, have been changed. The happenings at the Palace of the Nunciature, narrated by Mr. Aretal, are also autobiographical.[24] Following the pattern established by his first two novels, the interest of this work does not lie in what happens, but rather in the way the author artistically re-creates a series of simple and sometimes even vulgar incidents. Taken at face value, this is not a very exciting novel, but when it is read as an allegory, it becomes fascinating. Meruenda's life becomes a parable for what happens to man when he allows his animal side to dominate. His base nature puts him on a par with the lowest forms of life. From the very beginning of his delineation, Arévalo Martínez suggests Meruenda's physical resemblance to a pig; he first pictures him as fat, pink, and soft and as an indiscriminate glutton. Later Aldano receives the distinct and eerie impression that Meruenda has a beastly snout, a long, sucking, brutish snout (*Noches*, p. 27). The symbolism is rather obvious, since in practically all cultures the pig is the essence of uncleanliness and exemplifies the basest and most animalistic instincts in man. Meruenda's physical appearance is simply the outward representation of his impure spirit. Arévalo Martínez emphasizes this when he refers to Meruenda's soul as being a "foul-smelling manure heap" ("estiercolero hediondo"—*Noches*, p. 35). Meruenda allows his instincts to dominate to the extent that they have destroyed his spiritual side. As a man, Meruenda is the most abject of creatures. He exhibits all the attributes of a true degenerate: he is a glutton, a thief, a drug user, a sacrilegeous person, homosexual[25] (or rather, bisexual), and a gigolo. He has been endowed with a most precious gift, the ability to contact the world of the spirits, but his lack of self-discipline does not allow him to control his visions. He simply arouses disruptive forces that create chaos around him.

Aretal's lifestyle has several points in common with Meruenda's. He also indulges in drugs, and he is a homosexual,[26] but on the other hand, he is an intellectual who has learned to cultivate the spirit and who obviously is able to attain the right kind of mystical experience, helped in this case by Aldano's refined spirit.

Meruenda and Aretal can be seen as the two extremes between which Aldano's feelings are polarized. When Meruenda first arrived at his home, Aldano had just recovered from an operation and was reading the works of the Spanish mystical writer Saint Teresa (1515–1582) and meditating on the fact that being so close to death had heightened his desire to live. At that moment, his sensuality was as great as his fear of the unknown. He was so full of lust and terror that he had to put the book down to concentrate on his inner life. As he did so, Meruenda knocked at the door (*Noches*, pp. 7–8). From this moment on, the novel begins to develop the allegory about Aldano's soul. He is divided between the flesh and the spirit or intellect. Left to its own devices, the flesh turns any man into a Meruenda; with spiritual controls, he becomes restless and inquisitive like Aretal. And yet, no matter how refined man becomes, he can never be complete by himself. Aldano alone cannot find the answer to the riddle of existence. He needs the help of another refined spirit, and he finds it in Aretal. There are Neoplatonic connotations to the interaction of these two equally powerful and sensitive minds.[27] Aldano explains that meeting Aretal again is like finding himself

(*Noches*, p. 40). When they are together, Aldano forgets his family and Aretal his vices. They become omniscient—"Isis breaks her veil and the Sphynx speaks, opening a hole in the walls of mystery" ("Isis rompía su velo, la Esfinge hablaba, se abría un boquete en las paredes del misterio"—*Noches*, p. 41)—and eternal (they can glance back to the Athens of Pericles and see the future). They are two young gods (*Noches*, p. 44). The union, however, cannot be maintained because they are mere mortals and because Aldano-Arévalo's Catholicism, the fear of God's punishment, forces him to back away from any experience he considers sinful.

The Nights at the Palace of the Nunciature is the last novel in which Arévalo Martínez deals strictly with self-analysis. At the time he published this work he was forty-three, old enough to have come to grips with his own idiosyncrasies, and although he would still write autobiographical tales that show the continuous struggle going on in his soul, his novels, from this moment on, become a vehicle for social ideas.

These three novels, A Life, Manuel Aldano, and The Nights at the Palace of the Nunciature, are indispensable for an understanding of Rafael Arévalo Martínez's life and his contribution to Spanish American literature. They show the development of his morbid personality and the tremendous effort it took for him merely to survive, let alone triumph, in a world full of real people with real problems. His struggle produced experiences that were far from heroic in the ordinary sense of the word, but his suffering was very real, and he succeeded in making it the raw material of his art. The sincerity with which he exposed his soul, showing his most intimate emotions, thoughts, and reactions, was something new in Spanish American literature. New also was the direct and simple style, the lack of rhetoric with which he expressed his concerns. These elements were essential to the creation of an autochthonous narrative. Arévalo Martínez can thus be said to have contributed directly to the eventual rise of the new Spanish American novel in the second half of the twentieth century.

CHAPTER 4

The Narrative Of Political Commitment

SPANISH American literature is dominated by a prevailing concern for political and social issues. Men of letters, unable to evade their circumstances, have felt compelled to fight oppression, tyranny, and poverty with the best tool at their disposal—the political novel. Rafael Arévalo Martínez is no exception. Though *preciosismo* and narcissism were the main characteristics of his early works, with time his social concern became so acute that the critic Raymond A. Moody arrived at the conclusion that Arévalo Martínez's two major interests were "an introspective concern with the narrator's personal psychology, together with, and sometimes identified with, that of the people who are around him, and a social concern about man's place in society. While emphasis shifts back and forth between these two interests, there is a tendency for the second to gain in dominance."[1] It could not be otherwise. Given Guatemala's political and social backwardness and the prevalent climate of restlessness and protest, any conscientious person had to become involved in the fight to rid the country of tyranny and abject poverty.

The works analyzed in this chapter show Arévalo Martínez's preoccupation with social issues. They were published over a period of twenty years, but in spite of this range of time, their themes are similar. *La Oficina de Paz de Orolandia (Office of Peace in Goldland)*, a novel published in the twenties, soon after the overthrow of Manuel Estrada Cabrera's regime, describes the times and the fall of the dictator, while emphasizing the tyrant's subservience to Yankee imperialism. *¡Ecce Pericles! (Here is Pericles!)*, a biography of the same Don Manuel, and the novel *Hondura (Depth)* form a unit; both were published in the forties, after long years of research into the life of the dictator. In the preparation of these two works, Arévalo Martínez used his position as head of the National Library to read all available documents about Estrada Cabrera and his regime. Ironically, by the time the novelist finished his carefully documented

works, a new dictator was in power, and Don Rafael could not risk
publishing them, since an attack on Estrada Cabrera's tyrannical rule
would have been interpreted as a condemnation of the new regime.
Although all three works deal with anti-imperialism and dictatorship,
the manner in which they express those concerns is quite different.
Here is Pericles! and, to a lesser extent, *Depth* are serious indict-
ments of the country's corrupt politics, while *Office of Peace* satirizes
the Guatemalan government and American imperialism in a humorous vein; the situation portrayed its grotesque rather than tragic.

I   La Oficina de Paz de Orolandia

In the autobiographical novel *Manuel Aldano,* Arévalo Martínez
narrated how he first became aware of Guatemala's political problems.[2] Beginning with *Office of Peace in Goldland* (1925), subtitled
Novel of Yankee Imperialism, he vented his wrath at the demeaning
manner in which the United States treated the weaker republics to
the south.

Félix Buendía, the protagonist, is an unemployed writer who
succeeds in getting a job as reporter for the official publication of the
Office of Peace, the *Goldland Review.* He is so successful that he is
quickly promoted to editor and soon afterwards becomes the office's
secretary general. From that moment on, the novel's emphasis shifts
from the protagonist to the description of the unbelievably confusing
state of affairs that prevails at the office. The last seven chapters widen
the focus to allow the author to analyze the fall of the dictator Gabriel
Moneda Becerra (Manuel Estrada Cabrera) and the relationship of
the United States vis-à-vis Latin America's dictatorships.

The place of the action and the identity of the institution satirized
by Arévalo Martínez in this novel have been the object of some
debate and of several misunderstandings among the critics. Some
have associated them with a real institution and a real place: The Pan
American Union and Washington, D.C. Seymour Menton believes
that this novel traces, in a satirical vein, the history of the union from
its foundation in 1900 through the last meeting held in 1920.[3] This
opinion is shared in part by Thomas E. Holland, who agrees with the
identity of the institution but locates the action in Latin America.[4]
Kessel Schwartz, on the other hand, believes the Office of Peace to be
fictional. For him, Arévalo Martínez "satirizes imperialistic di-
plomacy" using the "mythical meeting place of a league of nations."[5]
The truth is simpler and more in accordance with the sources of

inspiration normally used by Don Rafael: *Office of Peace in Goldland*
follows his well-tried formula of mixing autobiographical and fictional
elements. He satirizes in this novel his personal experiences, describing his work for the International Central American Office in
Guatemala City. The "Office of Peace" was created to insure Yankee
political and economic interests in Orolandia (Goldland, the name
used by the author to disguise Guatemala). The administration of the
office was the joint responsibility of representatives of the five
Central American republics, and their comic inefficiency provides
Arévalo Martínez with some of the most humorous scenes in the
novel. He worked for the office five years (1915–1920), starting as
collaborator for its official publication, the magazine *Centro América*,
and moving up through the ranks to become its editor and the office's
secretary general.[6] The plot of the novel reproduces his successful
career within this unbelievably grotesque institution.

The protagonist, Félix Buendía, is another alter ego of Arévalo
Martínez. He is timid and easily intimidated, but in this instance, a
new and radically different motivating force has been introduced.
The protagonist may still be a shy, penniless poet, but he is married to
a pretty wife who dutifully adds a new child to their brood at regular
intervals. With the survival of his family at stake, the hero must
struggle to succeed at the office. At the beginning of the novel, the
situation closely parallels the circumstances depicted in the opening
pages of *Manuel Aldano,* but Arévalo Martínez is no longer interested
in psychological insights and character analysis. Instead, he concentrates on social criticism. Showing a superb flare for irony and
understatement, he ridicules both the United States' imperialistic
manipulation of Central America and the Latin Americans' inability
to rid themselves of their oppressors and to develop a life standard
comparable to that attained by Europe and North America.

The subtlety of Arévalo Martínez's scorn has led some critics to
miss the point of his rather vicious attacks. Thomas E. Holland
concludes that in this novel one finds "no hatred shown toward the
Yankee, nor does the author deluge the reader with incessant details
to demonstrate his thesis."[7] Holland's opinion is contradicted by
Arévalo Martínez's softly worded, but nonetheless devastating,
anti-American pronouncements. For Arévalo, the office is the symbol
of American imperialism and Latin American humiliation. He says,
for example, that above the chaotic local government, alone and
corrupted, stands the "unlikely Office of Peace, emblem of the
Yankee imperialism that created it and of the national disaster that

humbly accepts its imposition" ("inverosímil Oficina de Paz, emblema de la imposición Yanqui, cuya es su creación, y del desastre nacional, cuya es la aceptación humilde").[8]

One of the strongest passages in the novel condemns the subservient acceptance of United States control by Latin America. The passage deals with a visit to Goldland by representatives from both the Hispanic and the Anglo-Saxon cultures. Herrarte,[9] the ambassador of the Hispanic race, was on a tour of Spanish America, preaching national pride and solidarity against Yankee imperialism. The Guatemalan government scorns him because it fears that his acceptance would bring retaliation from the United States. Consequently, when the politicians learn of the reception that the office had innocently prepared in his honor they forbade it, and Herrarte could not, at the last minute, be received at his own party. Herrarte was not surprised by this action, which he saw as typical of what had taken place at every country he visited. The situation had been the same everywhere: the government and the oligarchy shunned him, but the people received him with open arms. Herrarte's visit to Goldland was followed one week later by the visit of Xpon, the Anglo-Saxon representative, whose job it was to mitigate the effects of Herrarte's preaching. Another reception was carefully prepared by the office, but this time the guest did not condescend to honor it with his presence. Casarrica, one of Goldland's delegates to the office, finally accepted the affront of his absence and made the following speech to his colleagues: "Do not be stupid, gentlemen! Xpon is not coming. So what? Xpon has Xponed in our face. His race also does it to ours. But, confound it! That is not going to kill us. Xpon! Let's uncork the champagne!" (¡No sean bobos, señores! Xpon no viene. ¿Y qué? Xpon nos hizo Xpon en la cara. También su raza se lo hace a la nuestra. Pero, córcholis, por eso no moriremos. Que salte ¡Xpon! el corcho del champagne. *Oficina*, p. 128). Arévalo Martínez's bitterness and shame cannot be more eloquently expressed. His pride in the accomplishments of his people is great, and he has difficulty accepting the secondary role to which they are relegated by the ambition of their own leaders who consistently back down in front of the North Americans' aggressiveness.

Arévalo Martínez accuses the United States of supporting any dictator who will protect American interests, even at the expense of the other nation's well-being. The novelist points to Yankee imperialism as the evil monster that hides behind the dictator Gabriel Moneda Becerra and allows him to reign supreme, at the expense of all personal freedom. In return, the tyrant must destroy anyone who dares defy the United States' right to absolute control of Goldland. The "rebels" are always appropriately punished: men of letters are censured; politicians lose their influence; industrialists are deprived of necessary raw materials; merchants lose their credit; and so forth (*Oficina*, p. 141).

In a long conversation with Félix Buendía, Casarrica, one of the five delegates to the office, defends an idea prevalent in Central America at that time. He believes that many of their problems would be solved if the United States simply annexed Goldland. Félix, on the other hand, defends the right of the Latins to be free and to compete with the United States for a better life for their people. He believes that so far the North Americans have led the race, but he condemns them because he believes just as strongly that the Americans are interested only in material progress. According to Félix, the future does not belong to the materialist, but rather to a people who will be a combination of Yankee physical power and Latin spiritual strength.

Arévalo Martínez's ideas throughout this section of the novel reflect his sympathy for the thesis of Latin America's humanistic superiority, prevalent among many of the Modernist writers. Rubén Darío, in his poem "A Roosevelt," had emotionally warned the American President against underestimating Spanish America, but perhaps the best defense of the Latin's claim to intellectual superiority is contained in José Enrique Rodó's well-known essay *Ariel* (1900), one of the most influential books in Spanish America at the turn of the century. His ideas seem to dictate Arévalo Martínez's optimistic promise of a better future, attained through the fusion of North American practicality and Latin American idealism.

Office of Peace in Goldland can be seen as a novel of transition. In it, Arévalo Martínez tried to reach beyond the strictly personal world he had presented in his psychological novels. For the first time in his narrative, social concerns took precedence over his morbid sensibility, but the novelist was still unable to detach himself completely from the protagonist. Therefore, Félix Buendía reacted to the world in very much the same manner as Arévalo Martínez. He was a sensitive writer making his first incursion in the world of politics, and he was shocked by it. His perplexed reaction is captured in the amusement and disbelief portrayed in the novel. The outright attack on the government and its institutions is softened by the humorous note, but despite the light tone used, it is evident that Arévalo Martínez was deeply concerned by the corruption of Guatemalan politics. The extent of the problems, however, would not become clear to him until he began to analyze the situation systematically, in order to write the biography of Estrada Cabrera.

II ¡Ecce Pericles!

The amount of investigation involved in the preparation of *¡Ecce Pericles! (Here is Pericles!*, 1945) is monumental. To piece together the history of how a dictator gains power and retains it against the desires of the majority, Don Rafael spent several years reading documents, interviewing friends and enemies of the ex-president, and gathering all available types of evidence. The result of his efforts is a very readable and impressively documented account of the life and times of Estrada Cabrera and, by extension, an exposition of the nature of almost any Latin American dictatorship.[10]

The biography is in two volumes. The first, subtitled *Manuel Estrada Cabrera,* has six "books," or parts, which deal chronologically with events of the dictator's private and public life. Book one, "Los primeros cuarenta años" ("The First Forty Years"), establishes Don Manuel's personality. The illegitimate son of a seminarist and a humble candymaker, Don Manuel grew up with an acute inferiority complex. Hard work won him the protection of Father Herrarte, a priest who allowed him to study without charge among the aristocratic pupils of a Jesuit school in the provincial town of Quetzaltenango. Don Manuel never forgot the disdainful attitude of his classmates, and they and their families would pay in the future for what were in most cases childish pranks magnified by Estrada Cabrera's sensibility. Don Manuel became a powerful provincial lawyer and politician. Eventually he was named secretary of the interior by President José María Reyna Barrios, whose assassination made Estrada Cabrera the acting president of Guatemala. Book two, "The Interim President," explains how Don Manuel changed the constitution in order to be nominated for the highest office in the country and how he later manipulated the election to win his first presidential term. Each of the next three books deals with one of his three consecutive presidential terms and provides ample proof of the reign of terror he unleashed on the unsuspecting people of Guatemala. The sixth and last book deals with the first two years of his fourth term. The second volume is subtitled *Cantar de gesta: Historia del partido unionista (Saga: A History of the Unionist Party)* and is dedicated in its entirety to an analysis of the birth of the opposition party and the role it played in the fall of Estrada Cabrera. Book one, "Las prédicas del Padre Piñol" ("The Sermons of Father Piñol"), studies this bishop's daring attack on Estrada Cabrera from the pulpit, an action that disconcerted the aging dictator and initiated the series of events leading to his overthrow. Book two, "Cien días de tinta," ("One Hundred Days of Ink"), emphasizes the role of the press in the foundation of the Unionist Party. Book three, "Y una semana de sangre" ("And One Week of Blood"), gives a day-by-day account of the dictator's bloody final week in power; his indecision and cruelty prolonged the struggle unnecessarily, producing countless deaths among the unarmed civilian population. Book four, "Después de la caída de Cabrera" ("After the Fall of Cabrera"), shows the aftermath of the overthrow and Arévalo Martínez's growing disillusion with politics. The actions following the tyrant's defeat lead Don Rafael to believe that the patriots fought in vain. The Unionist leaders were too idealistic and were, therefore, replaced as heads of the new government by practical but mediocre politicians who quickly thwarted the people's drive for freedom and democracy.

Here is Pericles! is not a conventional biography. Since Arévalo Martínez never attempts to give a fleshed out portrait of his subject, it is more the biography of a dictatorship. The whole emphasis is placed on the role of the man as a political animal; any details given about his growing years or his private life are provided only when needed to explain his ambition and his ruthless conduct. During twenty-two long years, everything in Guatemala moved at the will and whim of the dictator; he was the one and only motivating force in the country, and the motivation he offered was fear. From the highest government officials to the lowest peons everyone feared him. No one really understood him because his suspiciousness was such that he allowed no one to get close to him. When Arévalo Martínez asked one of Estrada Cabrera's closest friends to give the most salient characteristic of the dictator, the man responded with only one word, "mistrusting" ("desconfiado"). After further questioning, he gave six other traits that form a miniature portrait of the tyrant: "hermetic, spiteful, power hungry, endowed with leadership, persuasive, and a good talker" ("hermético, rencoroso, codicia del poder, don de mando, sugestión para los demás, hábil conversador"—*Ecce*, I, 25).

Estrada Cabrera did not tell anyone his feelings; neither did he explain his behavior to anyone: therefore, Arévalo Martínez does not attempt to record the dictator's point of view. Instead, the biographer presents anecdote after anecdote and example after example of

Cabrera's erratic behavior, his cruelty, and his injustice. As a result, the reader is as bewildered as were the dictator's subjects: everything he knows is hearsay and rumor. The dictator becomes an almost mythical figure; he is in control of everything, but out of the reach of everybody. The reason for his apparently whimsical actions, or even whether he was aware of their nature, is not always clear. The uncertainty adds to the horror of the situation, since it is hard to avoid doing the wrong thing when one cannot calculate what the right thing would be.

After establishing the character of the dictator, Arévalo Martínez describes the methods he used for attaining power. His actions during the presidential campaign already show all the political evils that would become more pronounced with time. The editorials in the periodical *La Ley (The Law)*, which defended the candidacy of a member of the opposition party, José León Castillo, are used by the biographer as evidence of the corrupt campaign run by the interim government. The numbers published from April 28 to July 26, 1898, give the whole sordid story. The following are some of the many intimidating techniques used by Estrada Cabrera's followers, the *cabreristas:* people who sympathized with the opposition were threatened, jailed, and beaten; the registrar refused to extend voting cards to members of the other parties; government funds were spent for the publication of partisan propaganda in Guatemalan and foreign newspapers; voters were kept locked up in corrals until they voted "voluntarily" in favor of the government's candidate; the army (in civilian dress) was forced to participate in pro-Cabrera rallies; thousands of false ballots were issued; the worst criminals were taken out of jail to bully and even kill the opposition (*Ecce*, I, 57–65). Understandably, the situation deteriorated into a reign of terror of major proportions.

Estrada Cabrera's long regime made a mockery of democratic practices. Through his dictatorial actions, he destroyed the balance of power almost beyond repair. The executive became the only power in the nation, since he effectively corrupted the legislative and judicial branches. During his first eleven months in office, Estrada Cabrera appointed most of his friends and supporters to the assembly. The few who were not his followers quickly learned that opposition to the president's wishes meant imprisonment, banishment, or death (*Ecce*, I, 81). The judiciary was as effectively destroyed by appointing to the benches anyone who supported the dictator. Judges were paid ludicrously low salaries, which they were expected to supplement by selling justice to the highest bidder (*Ecce,* I, 123–24). Teachers and intellectuals lost their right of free speech when the university lost its autonomy and became subordinated to the executive power (*Ecce,* I, 79–80). The situation in the public schools became so critical that teachers were paid only the equivalent of two or three dollars per month. Arévalo Martínez paints a sad picture of ragged children playing in dirty, broken-down classrooms supervised by drunken teachers (*Ecce,* I, 117–18). In sharp contrast, and mostly to be used for foreign propaganda, Estrada Cabrera, who had named himself "Protector of Youth," organized well-publicized yearly celebrations, called "Minerva Festivals," in which the country honored the glories of youth and the values of education (*Ecce,* I, 90–99).[11]

Estrada Cabrera's Machiavellian system of government intimidated the upper classes and allowed him to rule quite unchallenged for many unglorious years. But, if leaders and intellectuals suffered, the common people did not fare much better. Policemen and soldiers went hungry and unpaid, and in many cases had to steal in order to eat (*Ecce,* I, 59); manual workers and farm laborers had to work free for the government; at times they were forcibly separated from their families and locked in barracks to insure their collaboration (*Ecce,* I, 126–37). Those who protested ended in jail, where conditions were so horrible that it was better to end up in the cemetery. As a matter of fact, the most revolting sections in the book deal with the treatment of prisoners. It is hard to imagine that human beings could descend to such unbelievable depths of degradation in their relations with other human beings.

The "system" devised by Estrada Cabrera was based on his concept that man is ruled by his bestial instincts. In a conversation with Rodolfo Robles, the doctor of one of his sons, Cabrera explained why he trusted men who had been jailed by him and who had reasons for avenging themselves. Prison, he said, turned men into vegetables, then he added:

You don't know men; they are contemptible creatures; they can only be ruled with whips and boots. Have you ever realized the truth about the human condition? Those I have punished most violently were later my best servants. Have you ever noticed how people howl with bestial shouts when two women fight on the streets for the love of one man; when two poor laborers fight with their fists; when two cocks fight; when the bullfighter confronts the bull? Man only respects brutality and strength; and rather than other men he likes to dominate women and children.

Usted no conoce a los hombres; son criaturas viles; sólo se puede manejarlos
con el látigo y con la bota. ¿No se ha dado cuenta de la condición humana?
Aquéllos a los que más violentamente castigué fueron después mis mejores
servidores. ¿No ha visto cómo el pueblo da alaridos de gozo bestial cuando
dos mujeres se trenzan en la calle, disputándose el amor del mismo hombre;
cuando dos ganapanes se agarran a puñadas; cuando pelean dos gallos; cuando
el espada se enfrenta al toro? El hombre sólo siente respeto por lo brutal y lo
fuerte; y más aún que a los hombres se imponen a las mujeres y a los niños.
(*Ecce*, I, 386–87)

It is hardly surprising that a man with these principles would enjoy
brutalizing the country. What is surprising is that he was actually
right in his assumptions: by using the whip and the boot, he did
succeed in remaining in power for twenty-two years. This feat might
have been more difficult to accomplish had he not been backed by the
government of the most powerful and most democratic country in the
world—the United States of America.

The domineering role of the United States in Latin America has
become a commonplace topic, but it is a well-documented commonplace. Arévalo Martínez does not refer directly to the interfer-
ence of the Americans in the government of Estrada Cabrera, and
when he mentions actions clearly masterminded by them, he is most
restrained in his choice of words.[12] For example, he refers to the
establishment of the International Central American Office—the
subject of his satirical novel *La Oficina de Paz de Orolandia*—without
a word of bitterness. One might wonder about the wisdom of some of
the clauses included in a treaty of peace and friendship with Cabrera's
dictatorial government, but the author does not comment on this.
Neither does he comment on the irony that all the ideals espoused by
the office had been violated by Cabrera. Arévalo simply lists them: (1)
the peaceful reorganization of Central America and the unification of
teaching and laws; (2) recognition of the inviolability of life as the basis
for all legislation; (3) respect for private property; and (4) acknowledgement of the sacredness of human rights. Estrada Cabrera had
made a mockery of these ideals, but this did not deter him from
signing the treaty. There was a point, however, that did distress the
dictator: the clause that called for the nonreelection of presidents.
The objections were resolved to his satisfaction by citing the examples
of the United States and Mexico, where reelection to the presidency
was not considered irregular (*Ecce*, I, 250–52).

Arévalo comes close to condemning the American government in
the second half of the biography, where he deals with the superhu-

man efforts of the Unionist Party against Estrada Cabrera's regime. The rebels were peaceful men fighting a malevolent giant, and yet they could not count on any outside help. Father Piñol had been to the State Department in Washington, D.C., where it became clear that the Americans would not give moral support to the resistance (*Ecce*, II, 70); therefore, the Unionists did the next best thing: they pretended to have that support. They established their headquarters in a house next door to the American Embassy and spread the rumor that there were underground tunnels connecting the two buildings (*Ecce*, II, 95, 104, 124). Cabrera's intimidated henchmen were effectively deterred from either raiding the place or burning it down. They also selected the name "Unionist" for their party because the United States had backed the idea of a united Central America, and parties with this end in mind had been set up in some of the neighboring countries (*Ecce*, II, 73–75). They kept the American Embassy informed—through daily memoranda—of everything that happened, counting on the personal sympathy of the local staff. This was a sound practice, since at least on one occasion, the embassy intervened to save the lives of a number of Unionists about to be executed by the government (*Ecce*, II, 153–54), and it also admonished Estrada Cabrera not to harass the party's leaders (*Ecce*, II, 175).

The supposed understanding between the Unionists and the Americans offered a precarious security at best, and there were several crises that almost destroyed the party. At one point, the Americans told Cabrera that they would reaffirm their support of him if he promised to uphold the constitution. The president agreed, and the United States published, in all Guatemalan newspapers, a declaration of support of Cabrera against the "revolutionaries" that threatened his government (*Ecce*, II, 205–07). Later, when Cabrera was on the verge of defeat, the American delegation asked President Wilson to send ten thousand soldiers to reestablish peace in the country. Luckily for the rebels, Guatánamo Base could supply only three thousand. The dispatch of a greater number would have required congressional action (*Ecce*, II, 250–51).

In spite of American indifference to the Guatemalans' plight, the opposition prevailed and the corrupt regime of Estrada Cabrera was overthrown. The Unionist's triumph, however, was short-lived, for the idealism that had moved it had no place in the real world of Guatemala. Arévalo Martínez comments on the disillusionment that followed, a disillusionment based on the fact that in order to assume power, the Unionists had to compromise with the old regime. On the day the final agreements were signed, Julio Bianchi, the party's leader and the obvious choice for president, ostensibly stepped aside willingly, though he told a friend, "Freedom died in Guatemala today" (*Ecce*, II, 379).

Arévalo Martínez's disillusionment with the world of politics was so complete at this point in his life that it had a significant effect on his subsequent literary career, especially in his selection of themes. His interest now turns to an effort to shape the future of the world through his art, and the content of his later novels—the nostalgic portrayal of Guatemalan society in *Hondura* (*Depth*), the idealized civilization of *El mundo de los maharachías* (*The World of the Maharachías*), and the utopian society of *Viaje a Ipanda* (*Journey to Ipanda*)—may be assumed to have been selected, in part at least, as a reaction to the revulsion he experienced as a result of the preparation and composition of *Here is Pericles!*

III   Hondura

In *Hondura* (*Depth*, 1947) Arévalo Martínez experimented with yet another kind of commentary on the life and politics of Guatemala. The novel tells the story of Alfonso Celada, an unusually ambitious and determined rural youth. He was the illegitimate son of a poet from neighboring Honduras and a local country girl. Since he had to work as a child, he had no time for a formal education. One day the town's teacher gave him a dictionary, and the boy became obsessed with the idea of learning. He moved to Quetzaltenango to attend the local normal school and there met Father Lorenzo Castañeda, who was to become his lifelong mentor and friend. In Quetzaltenango, Alfonso fell in love with Magdalena, a regally beautiful girl five years his senior. When one of Estrada Cabrera's agents tried to seduce her, Alfonso was forced to kill him. He was jailed, accused of political assassination. Eventually, Estrada Cabrera freed him in the hope of being able to use him at some future time.

Upon regaining his freedom, Alfonso continued his one-sided love affair with the beautiful Magdalena, and now established in Guatemala City, he decided to become a lawyer and a writer (he eventually accomplished the first goal but never the latter, in spite of countless efforts at poetry, the novel, and the essay). This new facet of his life is narrated in twenty chapters that are a glorified account of Arévalo's memories of the colorful intellectual Guatemalan milieu of his youth. He described the student boarding houses and his personal relations with the writers of the period: Rubén Darío, José Santos Chocano, and Porfirio Barba-Jacob are among the most distinguished foreign artists with whom he associated, while Carlos Wyld Ospina, Flavio Herrera, Máximo Soto Hall, and Rafael Arévalo Martínez (who appears as a character under his own name) are among the many Guatemalan personalities mentioned.

The last fourteen chapters analyze Central American reactions to the first World War and to the creation of the League of Nations. The worldwide movement for peace and liberty that followed finally awakened the Guatemalans from their apathy. The long-suppressed patriotism and thirst for freedom burst forth, and a small group of conspirators, guided by Celada and others, led the people in the successful revolt against the tyrant.

The triumph of Celada opened up for him a brilliant career in government. At this point, however, he realized that his struggle for success had been motivated exclusively by his desire to win the woman he loved. When the now thirty-five year old Magdalena rejected him once again, he succumbed to his chronic weakness for alcohol and finally died in disgrace in a house of prostitution. Magdalena made the last sad comment on his accomplishments and character: during the funeral, her eyes filled with tears, she admitted to a mutual friend that she had always considered Alfonso a weak person, a man for whom she felt pity rather than love.

The action of *Depth* took place twenty or thirty years before the book was published, and it is obvious that the novel is a sentimental re-creation of the "good old days." *Depth* can perhaps be best understood if seen as a continuation and an antidote to the bitter, black world depicted in *Here is Pericles!* It is almost as if the novelist wanted to exorcise all the evils accumulated in the biography. *Here is Pericles!* had presented an absolutely polarized picture of Guatemala; it had shown human nature at its worst and at its most heroic. *Depth* gave a more balanced portrayal of the dictatorship: it showed that in Guatemala at the turn of the century there were other gradations than absolute good and evil, light and darkness; people were, after all, of human rather than epic proportions.

From the point of view of structure, *Depth* can be divided roughly into four parts, covering four widely different moods. The first begins when Alfonso Celada travels on foot from his home town to Quetzaltenango and to Guatemala City. The leisurely walk of the protagonist affords Arévalo Martínez the opportunity to exercise his descriptive powers; he renders highly impressionistic landscapes of the magnificent Guatemalan countryside and colorful and precise portrayals of the Indians he meets along the way. The settings he presents are bucolic and peaceful; the characters' actions, however, are those of the jungle. This section of the novel also contains an account of Celada's life as a student in Quetzaltenango and the story of his unrequited love for Magdalena, the girl whose defense costs him his freedom.

In the next section of the novel, Arévalo Martínez concentrates on the time the protagonist spent in jail; he presents a vivid account of the many horrors practiced in Latin American prisons against people whose only crime had been to displease a dictator. Many of the anecdotes had appeared in *Here is Pericles!*:[13] prisoners are abandoned for days in their cells, without food or water, and with their own excrement piling up at one end of the cell; merciless beatings occur, as many as five hundred *palos* ("blows") are administered for minor offenses; spies are planted among the prisoners to gather information; psychological terror is created by the constant persecution of innocent victims, and so forth. The characters in this section of the book are the paid agents of Estrada Cabrera, the thieves and assassins he kept as his personal agents in order to intimidate anyone he considered a threat or to get rid of the rich and powerful, whose fortunes he coveted. Together they made up the world of the hunters and the hunted.

The world of students and intellectuals described in the third section is perhaps the best part of the novel. These people seem naively happy and unconcerned with the political situation and the misery of the country. The students wasted their time making up funny Russian-sounding names for each other: a dark-looking boy was called Negrofoff, a bald one was Calvinich, a studious one Remachoff, and another with a particularly caustic nature was Toxinogüich.[14] They also spent many afternoons engaged in pointless, semiphilosophical discussions, dealing with the meaning of man and the importance of poetry, which they considered the only means of finding truth. They read poems to each other, and although they were sensitive enough to become highly emotional over a rhyme pattern harsh to the ear, they seem to have been oblivious to the horrors of torment and death that surrounded them. Their idols, Santos Chocano and Rubén Darío, were the worst examples in this respect: Chocano defended his friendship with all kinds of tyrants, claiming that they were mutually attracted because they were above ordinary men; they had been born to own the earth and were, therefore, above good and evil. Darío, suffering from alcoholism and half out of his mind, had accepted the dictator's invitation to come to Guatemala, only to experience frustration in his effort to write a poem laudatory of Estrada Cabrera due to the difficulty of rhyming his name. The tyrant, angered, retaliated by relegating him to a simple boarding house until the great poet, finally subdued, composed the poem (*Hondura*, pp. 109–14).

In this world of evasion and unconcern, World War I was to have an electrifying impact. Arévalo Martínez dedicates the fourth and last section of the novel to its analysis. The students and intellectuals, divided among themselves, debated endlessly the right of Germany (symbolizing brute force) to invade France (symbolizing art and culture). In 1917, while the war was still unresolved, a second event literally shook Guatemalan life: one cold December night, the earth trembled with one of the most severe of the country's frequent earthquakes. Everything came tumbling down: homes, churches, jails, schools. In the novel, both events symbolize the fall of the old order. The new age is heralded by the United States. First the young, strong American men took their vigor and their love of peace and liberty to Europe and freed half the continent from the brutalizing forces of Germany. Next their spirit came to Guatemala, where their dreams caught on among the intellectuals, forcing them to act. Estrada Cabrera, in the mistaken fear that the United States was backing the revolt, became vulnerable. He was afraid to act, and his indecision became his undoing. The students allied themselves with the workers and triumphed over the evil of dictatorship.

In *Depth*, Arévalo Martínez sees life as a constant struggle between opposing forces, a theme discussed repeatedly from different points of view by the intellectuals and the students. Each section and each sketch of the novel exemplifies the incessant confrontation of forces in the universe and within man. It is this theme that gives unity to the work rather than the more traditional devices of plot (which in this novel is decidedly thin) and character development (practically nonexistent). Arévalo Martínez justifies this technique of thematic unity in a discussion between Alfonso and Father Castañeda. The priest explains that a good novel should be like an album of sketches: the principal motifs represented in each vignette constitute the synthesis. He also believes that only the most significant scenes should be included (*Hondura*, p. 89).

The most obvious conflict in this novel is that between the two irreconcilable concepts of liberty and oppression. At the end of *Depth*, freedom conquers at every level. On a universal plane, the League of Nations will succeed in bringing peace to mankind; in Europe, civilization triumphs over brute force; in Guatemala, the dictatorship is overthrown in favor of a democratic government; and on a personal level, the protagonist, a weak man willing to sacrifice his principles, is defeated by the stronger character and the dignity of Magdalena.

Arévalo Martínez obviously includes in *Depth* a great deal of background material taken from his personal experiences. But the novel is not autobiographical, and therefore, it constitutes a clear departure from his previous tendency to identify with the protagonist. Celada's lack of principles, plus the fact that Arévalo Martínez appears as a character, weakens Kessel Schwartz's assertion that the protagonist is the author himself.[15] In *Depth*, none of the adventures in which Celada is involved actually happened to Arévalo. But perhaps the best indication that Celada and the author are not one and the same person lies in the fact that Alfonso is morally corrupt. He buys his freedom from jail with the implicit promise of collaborating with the dictator, and he allows alcohol and licentiousness to ruin his career and his life. In the other novels, the protagonists, Manuel Aldano and Félix Buendía, were physically weak, but they were honorable men, who bravely fought to overcome the tremendous problems presented by a weak constitution, poverty, and lack of recognition.

The more detached attitude toward the protagonist observed in *Depth* is indicative of Arévalo's growing concern with the world around him. The political novels analyzed in this chapter show this gradual change from a self-centered to a socially committed stand. During the first part of his life, his neurasthenia had blinded him to the intense suffering of his compatriots. When he finally began to look around him, he realized that there were other problems and that they were of such magnitude that they required drastic solutions. The solutions he first suggested, as seen in *Office of Peace in Goldland*, are not really solutions at all: he ridiculed the political structure, but instead of proposing a realistic program of reforms, he deferred to an improbable future race, purged of human faults, which would be able to create the ideal civilization. This naive optimism is almost entirely lacking in the rest of his novels. Time taught Arévalo Martínez several important lessons. On the international scene, the sobering experience of two world wars and the failure of the League of Nations and, at home, the never-ending series of dictators supported by Yankee imperialism were experiences that understandably diminished his youthful faith in mankind. Therefore, except for *Office of Peace*, his political novels begin to concentrate on proposing sensible answers that take into consideration human weaknesses.

CHAPTER 5

The Utopian Novels

THOUGH the discovery and conquest of Spanish America offered myriad possibilities for sociocultural innovation, one finds little utopian thought in that area of the world. According to Joseph L. Love, "Utopianism as an attempt to construct an idealized and rational communitarian society is a phenomenon almost totally lacking in Latin America. During the 500 years of colonial and national history in the region, one is hard pressed to find such movements. . . ."[1] He believes that except for religious experiments—the best known and most successful of which were the Jesuit missions in Paraguay—there were no organized efforts to bring about the implementation of the utopian theorists. Love lists a number of factors that, in his opinion, explain the absence of utopianism:

the existence of latifundium-based societies with many of the members of lower strata outside Western culture; the absence (until recently) of social stresses produced by industrialization; the course of Latin American political history, in which the problems of anarchy and tyranny absorbed the energies of the region's intellectuals; and perhaps a Luso-Hispanic "frame of mind," favoring doctrines in which social problems are placed in a cosmic frame of reference and for which utopian communities seem irrelevant—e.g. Thomism, Comtian positivism, and Marxism.[2]

Love's comments are basically true, but one must not forget that the majority of the people who came to Spanish America did not leave Spain because of political or religious dissent. For the most part, they were in complete accord with the principles of the Spanish government and the church, so much so that their aim was to re-create in the new world an exact replica of the models provided by the home country. Not the creation of utopias but rather the conquest of barbarism was the principle to which the early settlers adhered. Although the term "barbarism" was not coined until the nineteenth century, when Domingo Faustino Sarmiento used it in his well-

known treatise *Vida de Juan Facundo Quiroga: Civilización y
barbarie (Life of Juan Facundo Quiroga: Civilization and Barbarism,*
1845), the concept, as a way of life, had been present since the first
Europeans set eyes on America. All indigenous things were seen as
inferior and barbaric, and "civilizing" the Indians became the main
motivating force of the conquest. Unfortunately, civilization meant
"Europeanization," rather than a concerted effort to create a more
humane and spiritually advanced way of life. During the three
hundred years of colonial rule, Spain provided the sole model. After
independence, first France and later the United States supplied new
directions to follow, especially in the realm of ideas. As long as
Spanish America had readymade models worthy of imitation and
could blame native barbarism for its shortcomings, there was no need
to deal directly with their problems. The twentieth century, however, was to witness the decline of European and North American
prestige as models of modern civilizations. The negative aftermath of
the Industrial Revolution, with its blatant search for material progress and comforts at the expense of spiritual values, and the havoc
brought about by the two world wars forced many Spanish American
intellectuals to reconsider their position. As a result, a reevaluation of
Spanish America's potential and its possible contribution to world
affairs was started. The intellectuals, left without models to imitate
(Europe and North America having failed in their attempts to create a
better world), were forced to invent their own solutions. The time for
creating utopias had finally arrived.

Arévalo Martínez grew up and formed his ideas during these years
of self-appraisal. He had lived under one of Guatemala's most
tyrannical regimes and had analyzed and criticized the system in *Here
is Pericles!,* the biography of Estrada Cabrera. His utopian novels—
The World of the Maharachías, Voyage to Ipanda, and *The Ambassador from Torlania*—can be seen both as a direct result of his disgust
with the totalitarian forms of government and as a desperate effort to
warn mankind that, unless there were effective collaboration among
nations, the course of events made another world war inevitable.
These three novels constitute a drastic departure from the type of
literature Arévalo Martínez had previously written. They combine,
in a very imaginative fashion, what had been the author's two main
interests. Until this time, the psycho-zoological short stories and the
social novels had appeared as separate and distinct works. The first
had concerned themselves with the human psyche, analyzing character with a great display of fantasy, while the sociopolitical tales had

been critical of Guatemala's government. In the utopian novels, Arévalo attempted to combine effectively both trends in order to comment on the chaotic state of world affairs. The novelist presents the mythical Maharachías and their civilization with his characteristic imagination, while world politics and the social situation are analyzed with sound judgment and sensitivity.

I   El mundo de los Maharachías

The novel *The World of the Maharachías* (1939) ends with a postscript in which Arévalo Martínez pretends to offer some leads into the genesis of his utopian novels. Using a common literary device, he claims that he is not the author of this novel or of *Voyage to Ipanda* either: the manuscripts, he says, were reproduced using spiritualistic means; they are copies of old, lost chronicles, given to him by a young member of the diplomatic corps. Both accounts take place in the past, when all the earth's inhabitants lived on one large continent, Atlán, which preceded the mythical lands of Atlantis and Lemuria. Arévalo Martínez also refers in this postscript to Darwin's theories of evolution in order to justify the existence of an extinct superhuman ancestor of man endowed with a taillike appendix.

The action is narrated by Manuol, the sole survivor of a wrecked ship from the Lucíadas, a group of islands far removed from the continent of Atlán. The Maharachías, aware of the approaching extinction of their race at the hands of the warlike Dromonian people, decide to save Manuol, teach him about their civilization, and entrust him with a message for the future. While visiting their land, Manuol lives at the home of Arón and his two beautiful daughters Aixa and Iabel. The two girls represent the spirit and the flesh, and Manuol finds himself deeply divided between them. He finally chooses Aixa, who, because she has lost her tail, is the most human (hence the most imperfect) of all Maharachías, and the one who offers him love and peace of mind. They become engaged and enjoy a brief period of happiness, while he continues learning about the Maharachías mores. His education ends abruptly. One morning, Manuol awakened to find that all Maharachías had been assassinated. He himself is put in jail, where he awaits his execution, as the novel ends.

The World of the Maharachías deals with a completely fantastic situation, but the concerns expressed by the author are very real. He expresses them through the narrator, whose name, Manuol, is an unusual variant of Manuel, a name used by Arévalo Martínez several times before to designate his alter ego. The manner in which Manuol finds himself torn between the flesh and the spirit (Aixa and Iabel) is reminiscent of Arévalo Martínez's struggle to subdue his sensuality, a theme alluded to in most of his works. The author had used Manuel Aldano in his early works to reveal his most intimate feelings, while keeping his identity modestly veiled. Manuol is used in a similar manner to introduce, with some degree of impunity, his own political and social ideas and, more important still, to criticize the corruption of the Guatemalan government. He must have felt that it would be easier to side-step censorship if he wrote a novel about fantastic beings from a nonexistent land.

The Maharachías, except for their tails, had an almost human appearance. The extra appendage served as a kind of sixth sense and provided them with decisive advantages over the mutilated, tailless, human species. At first, Manuol was repulsed by their appearance, and he was quite overwhelmed by his contradictory feelings on meeting Aixa. Manuol explained that his first impression was an intuitive reaction of disgust. He justified his feelings by saying that all human beings loath anything alien which they do not understand. With time, however, Manuol came to consider Aixa and all her race beautiful:

I believed her to be an animal because she looked like a monkey. And she was superhuman precisely because she looked like a monkey! Ah! Later... Later what I loved most were her very small and shining eyes of sapphire, her fine eyes with blue reflections; her fine and thick blond eyebrows which contracted when she was deep in thought; her high cheek bones, which produced such mixed images in our first encounter.

La creía animal porque se parecía a un mono. ¡Y era precisamente superhumana porque se parecía a un mono! ¡Ah! Despues... Después lo que más adoré en ella fueron aquellos mismos ojos pequeños y brillantes como zafiros, aquellos ojos finos con reflejos azules; aquellas finas y pobladas cejas rubias que se contraían al paso de la inteligencia; aquellos pómulos prominentes, que en el encuentro inicial me produjeron tan compleja imagen.[3]

The three most important characters in the novel are Arón, Aixa, and Iabel. They represent the head (science and reason), the heart (love and feelings), and the fantasy of this exceptional race. Each had something valuable to teach Manuol. But perhaps the most important lesson he learned from them was that the creation of a perfect human society is an impossible dream. The Maharachías were perfect but they were not human. They had developed a harmonious civilization, which combined love of the land, work, and play in a wise measure. However, they were condemned to be destroyed by an imperfect, mutilated race. This represents an irony of fate difficult to understand unless one depends on the theories of Darwin: survival of the fittest means survival of brute force, a very negative message for those who hope that an advanced civilization could ever save human kind from barbarism.

Very few of the lessons that Manuol learned from this superhuman people are truly applicable to human situations. The novel, therefore, can be seen as another, and more imaginative, version of Arévalo's concern with the constant struggle going on in the universe between the forces of good and evil. In this particular case, evil seems to triumph. The novel, however, not only serves as an entertaining flight into the realm of fantasy, it is also an introduction to the world of the Ipandians, a superior white race with a very sophisticated civilization, developed with the help of the Maharachías, and because *Journey to Ipanda* takes place in the world of real man, it affords Arévalo Martínez the opportunity to trace parallels and to criticize specific political and social evils present in twentieth century society. He adduces implicit comparisons with the real world as he analyzes the conflicts raging within Ipandian society as well as the relationship of this country with the rest of the world.

II   Viaje a Ipanda

Viaje a Ipanda (Journey to Ipanda, 1939) is the story of the trip undertaken by Manuol to the imaginary country of Ipanda. This trip had been mentioned in chapter sixteen of *The World of the Maharachías,* where it was explained that it had been taken as part of Manuol's indoctrination into the accomplishments of Maharachían society. The two works form a novelistic unit in which Arévalo Martínez discusses his growing concern with the worsening political situation of the world. *The World of the Maharachías* presents a mythical country, inhabited by completely fantastic beings. Its society is depicted by a poet and a dreamer, and therefore, its accomplishments are not easily applied to human situations. *Journey to Ipanda,* on the other hand, deals with a real world populated by real beings. The message presented in this novel can be easily understood and interpreted as a warning to mankind. The author believes that unless nations and people learn to lay aside their narrow differences, the world will disappear in a holocaust made possible by the advances of science. Manuol, the narrator of both novels, is a man from a different race and from another country, shipwrecked in the land of the superhuman Maharachías. His saviors send him to Ipanda, a land inhabited by a superior, human, white race, in order that he may learn about the magnificent achievements Ipandian civilization has accomplished under its democratic government. At the time of Manuol's visit, Ipanda was at the pinnacle of its cultural development. But as often happens to a country at the peak of its power, this wonderful land was threatened by the envy and ignorance of the inferior races that inhabit the rest of the earth. The threat to Ipanda, the main supporter of the League of Nations, also entailed a direct threat to universal peace.

The main theme of this novel is the struggle between democracy on one side and the forces of tyranny and anarchy on the other. It is presented by means of a plot that mixes love and politics. The plot is introduced at the beginning of the novel and surfaces again at the end after the action has been much delayed by the detailed descriptions of Ipandian history and society. The plot is based on two love triangles. In one, Seda, daughter of Hernón, host and guide of Manuol and one of Ipanda's most respected citizens, falls in love with their attractive guest. Manuol, already in love with the Maharachían girl Aixa, cannot reciprocate, although he admires Seda immensely for her courage and is greatly moved by her delicate beauty. Seda's charms, however, awaken the irrational passion of Trémel (an anarchist leader of the emotional, inferior, darker races who live south of Ipanda), a person whose mere presence distresses the sensitive girl. In the second love triangle, Bolisario, the distinguished sixty year old ruler of Ipanda, is passionately in love with his attractive twenty year old wife Cota (also a member of the inferior darker races). Cota lives by her instincts. She is a sensuous and beautiful woman who cares only about herself and has put aside Bolisario in favor of her lover Hofernes, a leader of Ipanda's opposition party.

After the reader is informed of these facts, Arévalo Martínez proceeds to show Manuol engaged in the very serious business of gathering all possible information on the country, which is really the main purpose of his trip. In this section there are only a few casual remarks about the other characters to keep alive the reader's interest in the plot. Trémel's vain efforts to win Seda and Bolisario's growing jealousy of his wife's flirtation are mentioned, but the plot does not dominate again until the author finishes his detailed account of

Ipandian society. Then, at the end of the novel, the tempo picks up and the reader learns that on the morning when the fate of Bolisario's leadership of Ipanda was being decided at the Parliament, he received a message, sent by members of the opposition, announcing that his wife was running away with Hofernes. Overwhelmed by his personal tragedy, Bolisario fell easy prey to his political enemies and lost the vote of confidence he was seeking. Trémel, his formidable opponent during the critical discussion, won the debate, but he had also allowed his personal feelings to rule his life. As a matter of fact, his attack on Bolisario at the Parliament had been dictated by his frustration at having been rejected by Seda. After he destroyed his political adversary, he ran to the girl's house and, in a fit of passion, killed her and committed suicide. With these actions, two of Ipanda's most prominent leaders are eliminated: Trémel was dead and Bolisario had disgraced himself politically; with his personal life in a shambles, he was in no way capable of ruling the country. The third leader, Hofernes, also had allowed passion to prevail and, by running away with Cota, had abandoned his right to guide the people. This resolution of the conflicts leaves all private lives shattered and the future of the world menaced and uncertain.

Men's weaknesses had effectively endangered Ipanda and also the carefully designed charter of the League of Nations, a tool painstakingly put together in order to bring peace and order to the nations of the world. The league, in the long run, could be no better than the men who controlled it, and these men had now brought the world dangerously close to disintegration.

Ipanda's struggle for world power, which underlies the plot and forms the basis of the ideological framework of the novel, is presented in dialogue form by a series of characters who explain the history and the working of their society to Manuol. Each dialogue constitutes a small essay in which the author reveals different aspects of his blueprint for a utopian society. Unfortunately, the length and the didactic nature of these digressions diminish the appeal of the novel. The reader finds that the plot is only a thin excuse to present the author's political ideas. Though they are important ideas, they hardly justify the heavy dose of theory one encounters in *Journey to Ipanda*.

Ipandian society is idealized to show what the relations among men could be if they were truly based on charity and understanding. In a sense, the civilization described is the exact opposite of the Guatemalan society described by Arévalo Martínez in *Here is Pericles!*. In *Journey to Ipanda*, the author offers an antidote for almost every ill present in Estrada Cabrera's regime: (1) To replace the one man tyrannical rule of Don Manuel Arévalo envisions a democracy headed by Bolisario, a leader who respects parliamentary decisions. (2) The many political bosses, with absolute and whimsical power over life and death, are replaced by a Parliament with strong leaders, who help in shaping the fate of the country. (3) The counterpart of the corrupted judicial system of Guatemala is a most just and expedient organization in which, when incarceration becomes necessary, the prisoners are humanely rehabilitated in order that they may become useful citizens. (4) The disgraceful Guatemalan educational system is replaced by an enlightened method whereby teachers and students learn and progress together. (5) The crowded, inefficient hospitals, where the sick are treated like cattle or worse, are replaced by roomy and well-lighted buildings where patients are lovingly nursed back to health. (6) The demoralized army, made up of hungry, ill-clothed, illiterate Indians, has no counterpart in Ipanda—the only army is an internal police, respected by everyone, and the international divisions they contribute to the League of Nations. (7) Laborers, abused and poorly paid in Guatemala, are among the most respected and highest paid citizens of Ipanda. All these positive conditions and many others contributed to creating an atmosphere of trust and openness strikingly different from the fear and repression prevalent in Guatemala. It becomes obvious, after looking at the salient characteristics of Ipandian society, that Arévalo Martínez's careful analysis of Estrada Cabrera's regime convinced him that this dictator had created a grotesque, distorted picture of human society. He then felt compelled to produce his own version of the ideal civilization.

Arévalo Martínez's concept of utopia shows a considerable optimism in reference to the future of the world. However, the role that Latin America will play in that future is not too promising. Don Rafael's elitist spirit, a product of Modernism, seems to have prevented him from sharing in the hopes for the bright future of the racially mixed countries expressed by men such as José Vasconcelos (Mexico, 1881–1959) or Ricardo Rojas (Argentina, 1882–1957).[4] Contrary to these Spanish American intellectuals, Arévalo Martínez actually seems to believe in the innate superiority of the white, blond races who settled in the northern hemispheres. Even the Maharachías, those fantastic, superior beings he invented, were white. Although they exhibited some animal features and were physically closer to monkeys than to men, they had delicate features and blond hair. The Ipandians, the idealized version of men at the top of the evolutionary scale, are likewise pictured as strong, handsome specimens of the white race.

Arévalo Martínez makes occasional mention of white superiority in many of his books. In this novel, the references are continuous; the first Ipandian citizen Manuol meets is described as "blond, well proportioned, of handsome features and noble bearing" ("rubio, bien formado, de rostro bello y noble apostura"),[5] and the author explains later that in order to develop a refined family like Hernón's, "an evolutionary process of centuries is needed" ("la raza necesita haber caminado siglos"—*Viaje*, p. 15). Manuol's first contact with Ipanda gives him the impression that "the native race was intelligent, determined, and the possessor of a vast and superior culture" ("la pura raza indígena me pareció inteligente, tenaz y de una grande y excelsa cultura"—*Viaje*, p. 16). At the same time, he notices with delight their simple, almost primitive, characteristics that allow them to keep in very close contact with nature. The races to the south were in direct contrast with the Ipandian people. References to their inferiority are scattered throughout the book. Their problems were not caused by a lack of intelligence or even a lack of positive virtues, but rather by a lack of self-discipline, for they always allowed passion to rule over reason. Hernón complained that "the dreadful race from the south disrupts everything; it clouds the pure mirror of abstract justice with its breath of passion" ("la terrible raza del sur que todo lo trastorna; que empaña el puro espejo de la justicia abstracta con su hálito de pasión"—*Viaje*, p. 166). Their virtues and their vices are embodied in Cota and Trémel. Arévalo says of her: "she is the most beautiful woman on earth, or rather the most seductive. She came, like all our evils, from the south" ("ella es la mujer más bella de la tierra; mejor dicho, la más atrayente. Vino, como todos nuestros males, de las tierras del sur"—*Viaje*, p. 31). Trémel is also an attractive and impressive figure, one not easily forgotten. He exudes physical and spiritual strength, but he is also the portrait of violence (*Viaje*, pp. 23, 36). The passionate character of these races prevents them from understanding that the self-denying attitude of the Ipandians is a sign of inner strength rather than weakness.

At times Arévalo Martínez's racial comments seem almost gratuitous. For example, Bolisario explains at one point that Ipandians of all classes believe in their state and obey its laws; the only exceptions are among the immigrants, who are in large proportion dark-skinned people (*Viaje*, p. 166). The reference to color in this context appears unwarranted. The author himself seems to have been aware of his prejudiced attitude and at one point tried to justify it. After a bitter denunciation of the immigrants by Bolisario, Manuol asked him to comment on his observations about the colored races. Bolisario explained that his words were not meant to be scornful. Rather, he felt that he was stating a simple truth. To prove this point, he added that the worst immigrants were not necessarily the darker ones but individuals of a white and very intelligent race. He further believed that among the immigrants there were some excellent persons; the problem was that the majority were emotional people who were succeeding in destroying Ipanda's sacred traditions of democratic government (*Viaje*, p. 142).

The institutions so highly cherished by Bolisario exalted self-confidence and determination as the most important virtues in an individual. The country his people had created was ruled by an aristocratic democracy[6] where the masses recognized and accepted the leadership of those best endowed for that role and accordingly elected them to office (*Viaje*, p. 158). These leaders were expected to love the country above all else and to care for the people more than for their own lives. They had to be willing to sacrifice personal feelings at all times.

The people were treated equally and given similar opportunities for advancement. All work was regarded as worthy, and it was justly rewarded. The three most prestigious and best paid jobs were those of judge, teacher, and manual worker. The concepts of private property and the free enterprise system were recognized and encouraged, but the government set a limit on the amount of wealth any individual could accumulate.

Ipanda's educational system, like that of the ancient Greeks, emphasized a healthy mind in a healthy body. Sports and diversions went hand in hand with serious scholarly learning. When not playing, the students were encouraged to understand each subject to the best of their ability, rather than to memorize facts and minute details. Education was open to all; those who proved their intellectual capacity, if poor, were awarded scholarships to continue in school until completing the most advanced degrees. The only inequality in the system was that rich parents could conceivably pay for the education of a slow child, while poor parents could not.

The family was the core of society, and it was governed by the same civic virtues. There was mutual respect between husband and wife and parents and children. Each member respected the individual rights of the others. As a matter of fact, as parents grew older, they voluntarily divested themselves of many of their prerogatives in favor of their children. At one point, Hernón yielded to his son's advice, saying to the surprised Manuol: "—My son knows better than I. I respect him. His young cells think better than my old ones. His are open to a new life and are more sensitive to it..." ("—Mi hijo sabe más que yo. Yo lo respeto. Sus células juveniles piensan mejor que las mías viejas. Están abiertas a la vida nueva y son más sensibles a ella..."—*Viaje*, p. 26).

This wonderful country of Ipanda, democratic, liberal, and confident of the future, was behind the formation of the League of Nations and became its main supporter. The league's dream was to create a universal state to parallel the accomplishments of Ipanda, but its creators were realistic men who understood that humanity was not yet ready for this big adventure. They realized that some men were too nationalistic and selfish to give up their individual rights in favor of the well-being of the majority. Therefore, the league was created simply to police the world. Arévalo Martínez describes its foundation as the result of fear rather than cooperation. Bolisario addressed the leaders of other nations with these words: "I do not speak today to abstract ideas of goodness and justice, I appeal instead to fear and the instinct for survival. Let us not deceive ourselves; we are gangsters, and we represent nations that are assassins and thieves.... [therefore] I am not asking for just any kind of order, but precisely the order instituted by a band of thieves" ("Hoy no apelo a ideas abstractas de bondad y de justicia, apelo al miedo y al instinto de conservación. No nos engañemos; somos bandoleros y representamos a naciones asesinas y ladronas.... [Por lo tanto] No pido un orden cualquiera, pido concretamente el orden de una cuadrilla de ladrones"—*Viaje*, p. 126).

Bolisario, like any realist, was aware that men have weaknesses that are an obstacle to the creation of a social order similar to that of the Maharachías. Men can only hope to re-create a modified copy of the ideal civilization. The author makes it very plain that to aspire to pure idealism is an error. At one point Seda explains to an impatient Manuol: "My father already told you that in all human behavior one must always check with reality rather than obey rigid forms.... Why don't you abandon your idea of seeking the absolutes favored by your philosophers. ...?" ("Ya te enseñó mi padre que en todas las direcciones humanas hay que consultar siempre la realidad y no hay que obedecer a normas rígidas.... ¿Por qué no abandonas la idea de buscar siempre las cosas absolutas que priva en tus filósofos.

. . . ?"—*Viaje*, p. 186). The creation of the league is the implementation of Bolisario's—and the Ipandians'—realistic beliefs: since men will not live in harmony out of love and respect for each other, but will do it out of fear, then fear should be accepted as the basis for creating a society of nations.

When Arévalo Martínez mentions the league's problems in controlling the international relations of several countries, he is talking about historical facts. He modifies their names slightly, but it is not difficult to identify them. He makes direct references to the very serious political situation in Europe and Asia. Germona (Germany), Apia (Italy), Recia (Russia), Gracia[7] (France), Terra (England), and Opón (Japan) are the main contenders, and Hernón informs Manuol that the sympathies of the Ipandians are with Terra and Gracia. They admire these two countries because—as he says—freedom was born in the latter after having been conceived in the first one; they represent light, reason, and moderation (*Viaje*, pp. 157–58). Germona, Apia, Recia, and Opón, on the other hand, represent autocratic states, each interested in furthering its own aims at the expense of the authority of the league. Opón is an imperialistic country constantly engaged in wars of expansion (*Viaje*, p. 133); Recia has one of the worst forms of government in history: although it claims to be the dictatorship of the working classes, it is in reality the dictatorship of one party, which, to make matters worse, has become an immense and pitiless bureaucracy; Apia has another form of dictatorship: it is ruled by the bourgeoisie, backed up by a strong and well-armed militia; Germona has copied Apia's government and has gone one step farther by expelling its best citizens for racist reasons (*Viaje*, pp. 153–59). These countries understandably hated the League of Nations, which, by having outlawed war, had prevented them from engaging in their imperialistic designs. In a more vague and imprecise manner, the land of Ipanda is reminiscent of the United States. The problems the Ipandians encounter in dealing with democracy at home and abroad seem to parallel many of the situations in which North America found itself at the time Arévalo Martínez wrote these two novels.

Don Rafael seems to feel that in spite of all its faults, a powerful League of Nations is the best and perhaps the only way to curb the insolence of some countries. This optimistic view allows him to finish the book on a note of hope: As Manuol leaves Ipanda for the last time, he contemplates a spectacular sunset and reflects on the magnificent and eternal destiny of mankind.

III   El embajador de Torlania

Pedro Arce Valladares, in the prologue to *The Ambassador from Torlania* (1960), explains why, twenty-two years after the writing of *Journey to Ipanda,* Arévalo Martínez felt compelled to write again about the theme of utopia. Although by this time Don Rafael was seventy-six and much too old to travel, he was so concerned with the possibility of a third world war that he even considered going on a speaking tour through Europe and the New World. His intention was to publicize the need for the creation of a universal state. Eventually, he decided that writing a book might be more effective and the result was *The Ambassador from Torlania.* [8]

This last novel emphasizes once again the need for collaboration among countries, but Arévalo Martínez's literary treatment of the problem differs drastically from that used in his earlier novels. The most noticeable change lies in the direct presentation of the situation. The action takes place in contemporary times, and the struggle for power is between Russia and the United States. The opposing philosophies espoused by these two countries are defended by the antagonists, Rolando Decio, the ambassador and Russia's representative, and the narrator, Soveda, the representative of the United States. To remedy the unstable political situation of the world, America has decided to propose the creation of a universal state, a concept mistrusted by Russia.

The action takes place in a relatively short span of time and it amounts to nothing more than a play of wits in which each character tries to outsmart the other. The goal of the game is to gain approval of the type of universal state in which one of the member countries (Russia or the United States) will be able to dominate. Rolando Decio is a most attractive young man, not only handsome and successful in love, with all the dash and impetuousness of youth, but also brilliantly intelligent and cunning. He is most definitely a worthy enemy. Not as much is known of Soveda, the narrator. From his words and actions, it may be assumed that he is older, more mature, and wiser. He deeply admires Decio and plays a cat and mouse game with him in which he finally traps his antagonist. Soveda patiently sets out to gather the type of information about Decio's personality that will deliver him into his hands. He finds two highly incriminating items: he has written a love sonnet to a woman[9] (an unpardonable sin for any good Communist) and he believes in the power of reason. Soveda concludes that with these human weaknesses, if he feeds him the right information, Decio will eventually turn away from Marxist dogmatism. And he is right. Decio ultimately realizes the failings of his system, but he is destroyed by this realization. In learning the truth, he loses his youthful faith in himself and becomes useless to the Soviets, who abandon him and allow him to be assassinated.

A point of interest in the understanding of Arévalo Martínez's political ideas, although only of relative importance in this work, is the change of attitude the author has undergone since the writing of his first anti-Yankee novel. In *Office of Peace in Goldland,* he definitely felt that the United States abused its privileged position as leader of the continent, helped along by certain Latin Americans, who out of greed and ambition ignored its imperialistic maneuvers. In *The Ambassador from Torlania,* on the other hand, Arévalo Martínez thinks that the United States engages in a most benign form of imperialism, a kind of paternalistic overseeing necessary to both sides. This notion is expressed by Soveda during an argument with Decio. The American representative speaks of the fear of Soviet imperialism felt by the free world. Decio retorts, how about American imperialism? Soveda answers:

—It is not imperialism, except in the American tropics, where it is the most benign and civilized of imperialisms, compatible with national sovereignty and human freedom, and where not having it would be suicidal; we do not want godly virtues but human ones, that is to say, relative. It is an indispensable and necessary imperialism for those who exercise it; and saving for those on whom it is exercised. . . .

—No es un imperialismo, salvo en el trópico americano, en que es el más suave y civilizado de los imperialismos, compatible con la soberanía nacional y con la libertad humana, y en que no tenerlo, sería suicida; no queremos virtudes divinas sino humanas, es decir, relativas. Es un imperialismo imprescindible y necesario para los que lo ejercen; y salvador para aquellos en quienes es ejercido. . . .[10]

The author's reversal of attitude is not completely unexpected in view of his previous statements in reference to the inability of the darker races to understand democracy. His admiration for the accomplishments of the American people was consistent, although at times he lost patience with the arrogance of their government. Besides, in the struggle for peace and freedom, it became obvious to him that democracy, however imperfect, was a wiser choice than communism.

The Ambassador from Torlania deals almost exclusively with
Arévalo Martínez's unwavering belief in the need for a universal
state. The novel is almost a résumé of the ideas presented in *Journey
to Ipanda*. Gone are the detailed suggestions about setting up just
laws and democratic institutions in the new state. Also absent are the
narration of all novelistic incidents and the sidetrips which described
his utopic dreams in the earlier novel. Instead, the narrator syn-
thesizes the author's concepts in a series of conversations with Decio.
At one point, the ambassador told Soveda ironically that authors of
utopias ought to see a psychiatrist; Soveda responded with a concise
statement which summarizes Arévalo Martínez's ideas on the subject:

—This is not an utopia: this is a vital need; it is like a law which restricts the
homicidal instincts of men: law restrains the instincts that lead men to attack
each other and nations to destroy themselves. Men would have disappeared
without a state to give them rules for getting along with each other. In the
same manner, countries will die if the universal state does not come into
being and provide them with rules for getting along with each other.

—Esto no es una utopía: es una necesidad vital; es como la ley que restringe
los instintos homicidas de los hombres: es la ley que restringe los instintos
que llevan a atacarse y destruirse a las naciones. Los hombres hubieran
perecido si no llega el Estado, que les dió normas para convivir. De igual
modo las naciones morirán si no llega el Estado Universal, que,
análogamente, les dé normas para convivir. (*Embajador*, p. 61)

Obviously, Don Rafael firmly believed that mankind's only chance
for survival was to band together like a gang of highwaymen, just as he
had proposed in *Journey to Ipanda*. This concept is reiterated at the
end of the novel when Soveda thinks of Decio's last words to him. The
young man had said that, in theory, the need for the universal state
was absolutely logical—a truth as evident as the fact that two plus two
is four. In practice, however, he thought it was impossible to
establish it under present world conditions, although, perhaps it
would not be impossible in one thousand years (*Embajador*, p. 88).
Arévalo Martínez ends the novel on this positive note. He leaves the
door open to the future by suggesting that, despite the impossibility
of creating a universal state at this time, posterity will offer new
opportunities to mankind.

It has been said that "Behind the Utopias lies the utopian spirit,
that is, the feeling that society is capable of improvement and can
be made over to realize a rational ideal."[11] This spirit is not

altogether clear in the works of Arévalo Martínez. The novelist sets the action in the past, in a society that comes closer to representing a lost Arcadia[12] than a utopian society of the future, established after mankind had attained a more perfect and "civilized" understanding of itself. Thus, Arévalo Martínez seems to be saying that man, Darwin's theories notwithstanding, is retrogressing, at least as far as his humane qualities are concerned. In *The World of the Maharachías,* as well as in *Journey to Ipanda,* refined civilizations based on the highest principles of pure democracy are brought to an abrupt end by the envy of barbaric hordes of ignorant and emotional people. The men who triumph are always depicted as racially inferior. In all cases, barbarism wins out over civilization and refinement. The world, in his view, is destined to perish at the hands of the least capable species of mankind. The destruction is allowed by the superior race, whose high principles become their undoing; although aware of the impending doom, they will not use force or break down their democratic ideals in order to stop the enemy. He warns that in a less than perfect world, high ideals become the tragic flaw of all pure democracies.

The truth of his warning became apparent when the European conflict broke out in 1939 and was followed by the entry into the war of Japan and the United States. In spite of the high toll of death and destruction, World War II had no more of a sobering effect on mankind that any other war ever had. This fact must have been quite discouraging for the novelist. And yet he did not give up: in his novel *The Ambassador from Torlania,* he tried once more to warn the world that it was once again headed for disaster. Barbarism he now identified with communism, a threat the American continent began to feel closer to home when Fidel Castro and his leftist sympathizers took over Cuba. Arévalo Martínez warns the Spanish Americans to side with freedom in order to keep Western civilization intact. The resolution of this novel leaves no doubt of his optimism in reference to the outcome of this particular struggle and the continuation of man on earth.

CHAPTER 6

A New Concept In Brief Fiction

I *The Psycho-Zoological Short Stories*

ARÉVALO Martínez's most important contribution to Hispanic letters is the invention of the psycho-zoological narrative, the effect of which was to revolutionize the concept of the short story as well as that of the psychological portrait. The essence of the invention is to present the physical and psychological traits of the characters, most of whom were friends or acquaintances of the author, by identifying them with animals that exemplify their salient characteristics. Plot and action, elements that had traditionally dominated the short story, are subordinated to character analysis, and since each person is seen through the eyes of the narrator, the resulting portrait is distinctly subjective and original, and it is expressed in the artistic language that was the hallmark of Modernism. Some critics hold that it is this harmonious combination of carefully wrought prose and powerful interior vision that makes of Arévalo Martínez's psycho-zoological stories an effective bridge between the artistic novel of the nineteenth century and the psychological narrative of the twentieth.[1]

Detailed psychological analysis, carried to the extreme of revealing his most intimate impressions, is the essence and substance of Arévalo's narrative. This technique is effectively established in his first published story, "Wife and Children" (1909) and reaffirmed in his first autobiographical novel, *A Life* (1914). In 1915, with "The Man Who Looked Like a Horse," the range of this narrow autobiographical approach was widened to allow the participation of a second protagonist. The psycho-zoological stories differ from his previous works only in that the protagonist is no longer the author-narrator; he is, however, still an active participant, since the other character exists only in reference to him, as has been noted by Chris L. Dubs, who explains that " 'El hombre que parecía un caballo' seems to have set the pattern that the author was to follow in his later psycho-zoological narratives. This is to say, the tale is related in the first person, in this case by an unnamed narrator; also the protagonist is described by the narrator primarily in terms of his relationship to him."[2]

Since the characters are described from the narrow perspective of the portrayer, the portrait can be shocking to those who do not observe the subjects from the same angle. This personal approach is not surprising, since at this time the genre of the literary portrait was undergoing the same type of revolutionary changes that had been shaking up every aspect of literature since Rubén Darío introduced Modernism. The Nicaraguan poet, who changed so many literary stereotypes, had popularized his own brand of highly subjective literary portraits in *Los raros* (*The Eccentrics*, 1896). From that time on, many artists everywhere in the Hispanic world portrayed each other using the same unaccustomed techniques and points of view used by Rubén Darío. Another very original writer of portraits was Juan Ramón Jiménez, who, as suggested before, had an artistic temperament very similar to Arévalo Martínez's. In 1914, Jiménez wrote his first "lyrical caricature," a controversial type of subjective description destined to give a new orientation to literary portraits. His caricatures are so startling that, in spite of their significance to the development of the genre, he has been accused of lack of objectivity: the critic Damián Carlos Bayón is typical in his praise of Juan Ramón's style and psychological insights and in his criticism of the form. His main objection is that the subject is caught off guard and that only one aspect of his personality is given, making it representative of his total physical and psychological makeup.[3] Similar objections can be made to Arévalo Martínez's approach, but one must keep in mind that an artist is entitled to the freedom to express himself with originality. Don Rafael's point of view and technique may have been different, but his portrayals had an accuracy that is demonstrated by the fact that Barba-Jacob, the subject of "The Man Who Looked Like a Horse," was the first to recognize himself in the persona. Arévalo, however, does not seem to have been sure that the psycho-zoological type of character analysis would be well received, because in most cases he did not disclose the names of the subjects, who were only later identified by the critics.

Characterizations based on similarities between men and animals, which have been common in literature since antiquity, have traditionally attributed to animals human characteristics and customs while the animals clearly remain animals. Arévalo Martínez essentially does the opposite—his human beings are given the physical mannerisms and spiritual attributes of certain animals but they do not, clearly, cease to be human beings.[4] In the words of Professor Dubs, "In Arévalo's major animal narratives the protagonist does not physically possess any animal parts; rather, he has the movements and actions of the animal that the narrator perceives. There are also certain psychological characteristics of the protagonist that bring an animal to the mind of the narrator."[5] Professor Dubs also observes that, "Though other literatures present man and animal in the same character, Arévalo's personages do not undergo a metamorphosis, as do most other man-animal creations; that is, they do not change from man to animal or vice versa. Nor are they anthropomorphic, a common literary device wherein animals are given human characteristics."[6]

Given the uniqueness of Arévalo Martínez's approach, it is interesting to speculate on the reasons for his having chosen this particular form of portraiture. That he always had a keen eye for seeing the animal side of people is obvious; his books are filled with such references.[7] That literature abounds in man-animal comparisons is obvious also. Arévalo Martínez's use of this motif is so different, however, that it suggests a possible influence of the concept of the *nahual,* a deep-rooted tradition among the Indians of Central America.[8] According to Indian lore, each man has a double, a totem animal, which protects him and keeps him tied to the earth and the cosmos.[9] Contrary to normal Judeo-Christian symbolism, the animal does not represent man's base nature, but rather his natural instincts (the instincts of man prior to his original sin). The *nahual* is an essential tie between man and the universe, which the Indians believe has been lost through civilization and the mechanization of modern society.[10] In the context of the *nahual* concept, Arévalo's identification of man with animal could have no pejorative connotation, but consideration of his technique within that context is illuminating in that what he achieves—the penetration of his subject and the capture of his very essence—could be interpreted simply as the identification of the *nahual,* the double that marks a person indelibly with its own vital traits.

From among Arévalo Martínez's many psycho-zoological stories, only four will be examined here. The first three are included because they are representative of his art in a number of ways: "The Man Who Looked Like a Horse," was the first, and to many critics the best, of his animal cycle, and it set the pattern for the rest. "El trovador colombiano" ("The Colombian Troubadour") is a companion to the first story, and as such it expands on the portrayal of the man-horse. It is also an example of Arévalo Martínez's practice of reintroducing the same character in story after story. "Las fieras del trópico" ("The Wild Beasts of the Tropics") not only offers a magnificent analysis of the prototype of the Latin American dictator, but also shows the author's early concern with sociopolitical topics. The last short story analyzed, "La signatura de la esfinge" ("The Mark of the Sphynx"), though it was written almost twenty years after "The Man Who Looked Like a Horse," is included in this study because of the imaginative treatment of the complex character of its female protagonist, the Chilean poet Gabriela Mistral. Arévalo's fascination with her personality was such that he continued her analysis in several other stories: "La Farnecina," "El hechizado" ("Bewitched"), and "Complejidad sexual" ("Sexual Complexity").

II *"El hombre que parecía un caballo"*

"The Man Who Looked Like a Horse" (1915), Arévalo Martínez's first psycho-zoological tale, appears in practically every anthology of Spanish American short fiction. It deals with the relations between the author-narrator and Mr. Aretal—in real life his friend the Colombian poet Porfirio Barba-Jacob.[11]

The narrator's first subconscious impression of the protagonist is a vague awareness that Mr. Aretal's pose reminds him of a horse. However, he quickly forgets this image, falls under the spell of Aretal, and watches him display his "intimate" treasure of amethysts, emeralds, and opals (symbols of Aretal's magnificent poems). Fascinated by this dramatic performance, the narrator's spiritual antennae immediately stretch out to feel this new person, while he confesses to himself (in an interior monologue) that this is the man he has awaited so long. Next, the narrator figuratively spreads out his "peacock tail," hoping to impress his new friend. He succeeds, and Aretal allows him to look into his soul, an action that opens the door to a close relationship. Arévalo uses the image of fire to portray their feelings and the almost mystical transcendence attained through their friendship: "I burned and Mr. Aretal saw me burn. In marvelous harmony, our two atoms of hydrogen and oxygen had come so close together that, elongating themselves, emanating portions of themselves, they almost became one, in something alive" ("Yo ardí y el señor de Aretal me vió arder. En una maravillosa armonía, nuestros dos átomos de hidrógeno y de oxígeno habían llegado tan cerca, que prolongándose, emanando porciones de sí, casi llegaron a juntarse en alguna cosa viva").[12]

Soon, however, Aretal's horse image interfered. Each successive day and each change of mood produced a vision of the protagonist as a different kind of horse. Eventually the narrator realized that Aretal had no true personality; rather, he merely reflected the spirit of those who came in contact with him. He was completely amoral. The narrator suspected that the Aretal who fascinated him did not exist; he had been attracted only by the reflection of his own spirit in the protagonist. He posed this question to Aretal, who responded: "—Yes: it is true. To you who love me, I show only the best part of myself. I show you my interior god. But, it is painful to say this, between two human beings who surround me, I tend to take the color of the baser one. Run away from me when I am in bad company" ("—Sí: es cierto. Yo, a usted que me ama, le muestro la mejor parte de mí mismo. Le muestro mi dios interno. Pero, es doloroso decirlo, entre dos seres humanos que me rodean, yo tiendo a colorearme del color del más bajo. Huya de mí cuando esté en una mala compañía"—*Hombre*, p. 21). This admission of amorality on the part of the protagonist ends their friendship. Aretal, realizing that the narrator has captured his true essence, "kicks" him on the forehead and quickly "gallops" away.

This fascinating short story has been analyzed from every conceivable angle and praised lavishly by creative writers and critics alike. Rubén Darío, normally rather frugal in his applause of fellow Spanish American artists, after reading this work said of Arévalo: "He is neither Poe nor Lorraine, he is something new and marvelous" ("No es Poe ni Lorraine, es algo nuevo y maravilloso").[13] Gabriela Mistral (1889–1957), Chile's Nobel prize winner and an ardent admirer of Arévalo's works, wrote him a letter praising him in the following terms: "What a fascinating talent does Central America have in you! . . .You are a living classic, as fine a mind as Darío's. . . . Your *Man Who Looked Like a Horse* is one of the perfect readings that life has afforded me; your poetry was already an old friend of mine." ("¡Qué talento tan fascinante tiene en Ud. su Centro América! . . . Ud. es un clasico vivo, una mente tan fina como la de Darío. . . . Su *Hombre que parecía un caballo* es una de las lecturas perfectas que me ha dado la vida; sus versos eran ya vieja estimación mía").[14]

Literary critics have concurred with creative writers in acclaiming this work as one of the most powerful and original expressions in

Spanish American literature. The prestigious Spanish professor Federico de Onís said:

> The reading of a short story, "The Man Who Looked Like a Horse," and another one, "The Columbian Troubadour," left in me the unique impression of being confronted with a great writer. It was not a matter of the showy and superficial innovative ostentation, so often found among the young writers of Spanish America, but of a simple and profound originality.

> La lectura de un cuento "El hombre que parecía un caballo", y otro, "El trovador colombiano", dejó en mí la impresión inequívoca de hallarme ante un gran escritor. No se trata de alardes vistosos y superficiales de innovación como a menudo se encuentran en jóvenes escritores de Hispano América, sino de una sencilla y profunda originalidad.[15]

The well-known Chilean critic, Arturo Torres Ríoseco, commented with equal enthusiasm: "Arévalo Martínez is a true artistic temperament. Taking into consideration his sensibility and his power of aesthetic divination alone, I would dare say that Arévalo Martínez is the best endowed writer in our continent" ("Arévalo Martínez es un verdadero temperamento de artista. Tomando en cuenta sólo la sensibilidad y el poder de adivinación estética, me atrevería a decir que Arévalo Martínez es el escritor mejor dotado de nuestro continente").[16] The North American critic Seymour Menton, in a letter to Don Rafael, assigns him a leading place in Spanish American literature:

> It seems to me that in the development of the Spanish American short story, you play the indispensable role of having discovered the importance of internal reality. In your short stories the internal world of your characters stands out above the external world, perhaps for the first time in the history of Spanish American letters.

> Me parece que en el desarrollo del cuento hispanoamericano, usted hace el papel indispensable de descubrir la importancia de la realidad interior. En sus cuentos el mundo interior de sus personajes descuella por encima del mundo exterior, quizás por la primera vez en la historia de las letras hispanoamericanas.[17]

The predilection shown by creative artists and critics for this particular short story was shared by its author. Arévalo Martínez was fascinated by his creation and analyzed it several times in an effort to

explain the creative process. The aspect of this tale that has attracted
most attention from the critics is the manner in which the author uses
magic and fantasy to delineate the personality of the protagonist.
Opinions about the meaning of his multifaceted character have
tended to cluster around two main theories. One maintains that the
personality being developed is that of the protagonist Mr. Aretal, in
real life the poet Porfirio Barba-Jacob—whose strange behavior in
this tale is seen by some critics as pointing to a possible homosexual
relationship between him and the author-narrator. The other theory
holds that this story shows the development of the personality of the
narrator himself, who uses this technique to focus attention on the
two levels of his personality and of man in general: his spirituality and
his animality.

The first person to recognize the identity of Aretal, and to
popularize the homosexual theory, was Barba-Jacob himself. It seems
that he knew it even before the author, for Teresa Arévalo says that
when her father wrote the story he was not aware that he was writing a
description of the Colombian poet. [18] She says that Don Rafael, in a
flush of enthusiasm for the work he had just finished, hastened to read
it to his friend Barba-Jacob, who, after hearing the tale, jumped up
and paced the floor frantically, confessing all his vices and begging
Arévalo not to publish it, since obviously he was the protagonist and
the story clearly revealed his depraved nature. [19] According to Don
Rafael, he was not aware of his friend's homosexuality until that
moment. His assertions notwithstanding, the concept that there was
a relationship between the narrator and the protagonist has gained
wide support. Its most ardent proponent is Raymond A. Moody, who
insists that in the protagonist "ostentation and homosexuality are the
most obvious personality characteristics and they point toward an
intense egocentricity, which blocks out the possibility of more normal
human behavior and relationships."[20]

The second theory, that is to say, the theory that sees in Mr. Aretal
not an independent character, but rather another aspect of the
personality of the author-narrator, was also advanced by the critics
very early. The Guatemalan Carlos Wyld Ospina, just a few days after
the publication of the short story, said of the author: "by describing
the movements, either visible or internal, of the man who looked like
a horse, he had done nothing but portray his own personality: with his
spiritual highs and lows, his cruel and maniacal strokes of genius; one
more baring of a spirit that knew no shame!" ("al reflejar los

movimientos visibles o interiores del hombre que parecía un caballo no había hecho más que expresarse así [sic] mismo: con sus altitudes y pequeñeces espirituales, sus crueles genialidades de maníaco; ¡una desnudez más de su espíritu que no conocía el pudor!").[21] This opinion is shared by many critics. Daniel R. Reedy speaks for them when he says:

Mr. Aretal and the narrator are in reality one man, with Aretal in the role of a representation of the inferior or subconscious side of the narrator's psyche. Aretal represents the lowest, most instinctive and animalistic side of man, while the narrator is the superior side of the psyche—the moral, cultivated, and noble side.

el señor de Aretal y el Narrador son en realidad un solo hombre con Aretal en el papel de una representación de la parte inferior o subconsciente de la psiquis del Narrador. Representa Aretal la parte más baja, instintiva y animal del hombre, mientras el Narrador es la parte superior de la psiquis—la parte moral, culta y noble.[22]

Don Rafael's own view is in sharp contrast to that of the critics. He dealt with this subject repeatedly in his narratives, in statements to his daughter and critics, and in his essays. Especially intriguing is a small piece entitled "Porfirio Barba-Jacob,"[23] in which he treats the genesis of "El hombre que parecía un caballo," as well as its meaning, clarifying, and sometimes contradicting, details previously cited by himself and by the critics.

Arévalo Martínez believes that the identity of Mr. Aretal is completely irrelevant for understanding this short story. He reiterates that he did not realize who his model was when he composed it and that if he used Barba-Jacob, he did so unconsciously. He quotes a letter he wrote to the Colombian poet in which he reproaches him for boasting of being the protagonist of his tale; furthermore, he reminds him that an artist only uses reality as a point of departure for flights into imagination.[24]

According to Arévalo Martínez, despite the fact that the real meaning of "El hombre que parecía un caballo" is clearly expressed in two key passages of the text, no one has seen it, let alone explained its significance. He adds that the story was created under very odd circumstances. It came to him like a flow of electricity, which caught his spirit on fire ("como el flujo de una corriente eléctrica, que incendió mi espíritu").[25] As a result, he wrote the story in a trance, and he

confesses that he has never been able to explain to himself how he did
it. He is, however, very sure of the meaning of the two key
paragraphs. The first one reads:

—This is the man you were waiting for; this is the man you were seeking in
all the unknown souls you looked into, because your intuition had assured
you that one day you would be enriched by the coming of this unique being.
The eagerness with which you took, absorbed, and cast away so many souls
that made themselves be desired by you and defrauded your hopes, will be
completely satisfied today: lean over and drink from this water.

—Este es el hombre que esperabas; éste es el hombre por el que te
asomabas a todas las almas desconocidas, porque ya tu intuición te había
afirmado que un día serías enriquecido por el advenimiento de un ser único.
La avidez con que tomaste, percibiste y arrojaste tantas almas que se hicieron
desear y defraudaron tu esperanza, hoy será ampliamente satisfecha: inclí
nate y bebe de esta agua.

For Don Rafael, the meaning of this passage is obvious, because to
him the coming of this unique being can only be the coming of God.
The second paragraph reads: "Besides, the soul of Mr. Aretal was no
longer blue like mine. It was red and flat like the one of the comrade
who was waiting for us. Then I understood that what I had loved in
Mr. Aretal was my own blue!" ("Además, el alma del señor Aretal ya
no era azul como la mía. Era roja y chata como la del compañero que
nos esperaba. ¡Entonces comprendí que lo que yo había amado en el
señor de Aretal era mi propio azul!").

Arévalo clarifies that these words are the equivalent of saying that
the Supreme Being can be found within the depths of each human
being ("el Ser Supremo se encuentra en lo más profundo e íntimo de
todo ser humano")[26] and leaves no doubt that for him the essence of
his short story is this discovery that God was within him. The rest of
the tale he dismisses as literary trappings. He believes that the
descriptions of Aretal's personality and his personal relations with the
narrator are simply the framework needed for dealing with the theme
of self-knowledge. In defense of the critics, however, it must be said
that the anecdote seems to be based on autobiographical details.
Barba-Jacob's strange hold on Arévalo is confirmed by the fact that
Arévalo had attained another type of mystic-pantheistic union
through the mediation of the Colombian poet, an experience described in the novel The Nights at the Palace of the Nunciature.[27]

The search for a Supreme Being and the discovery that He is

already in each man is a theme found among many other Modernist writers.[28] It is essentially a lyrical theme which Arévalo Martínez succeeds in incorporating into the narrative. The formal and thematic perfection of "The Man Who Looked Like a Horse" shows how adept he had become at casting his interior visions into tangible images.

III   *"El trovador colombiano"*

"The Colombian Troubadour" forms a unit with "The Man Who Looked Like a Horse"; hence, Arévalo Martínez had them bound together in the same volume. Its subject is León Franco, another Colombian poet and a friend of Barba-Jacob, whom the author-narrator associates with a Newfoundland dog.

The narrator discusses several kinds of men-dogs, commenting on their vices and virtues, before concentrating on the protagonist, whom he sees as a "sweet family dog" ("dulce perro familiar"— *Hombre,* p. 31), a poor, common dog whom he considers the poet of the species and, for this reason, slandered by everyone *(Ibid.).* León Franco quickly becomes the narrator's friend. Arévalo explains that dogs always know how to recognize a friend; therefore Franco, seeing that he was an honest man, barked and leaped up to win his friendship. The tale continues with a series of anecdotes showing several other canine aspects of Franco: Franco when singing is depicted as a fat dog who has swallowed a linnet; Franco at the time of the siesta is a tired dog, sleeping or walking lazily with his tail down and his head lowered; Franco on an outing in the country barks and jumps around playfully before lying down quietly at the feet of the narrator.

At a party in Aretal's apartment the narrator, inebriated more by the distinguished company than by the alcohol, allows his own animal spirit to show—he is a sorrowful crane, one who feels grateful for being accepted by the refined souls present in the room. However, León Franco, who is among the guests, interrupts the fantasies of the narrator, who then makes the others admit that Franco is a dog. The day following this unmasking, Franco decides to leave the country. In the final scene, he begins to trot away, runs back toward Aretal and the narrator, howls in pain, and disappears down the street.

Although this short story lacks the structural unity of "The Man Who Looked Like a Horse," it is a fascinating study of another type of character—the humble, friendly expatriate, a true stray dog. At one point, the narrator playfully asks him a series of rhetorical questions (rhetorical in the sense that dogs are not expected to answer): Have you ever loved? Have you ever worked? What do you want . . . ? The unanswered questions lead the narrator to conclude that Franco is a real tramp, a completely useless dog (*Hombre,* p. 43). The story expands on Aretal's animal nature and shows him in relation to other characters. Arévalo also reiterates the almost mystical experiences he shared with the man-horse, explaining that any conversation they started always ended with a discussion of God, a subject so absorbing that they lost contact with the external world.

Perhaps the most interesting aspect of this short story is the narrator's presentation of himself as a crane. His deep-rooted inferiority complex is obvious in the symbol he chooses for himself as well as in his descriptions of his feelings. He is the poor soul of a bird, with mutilated wings, hating contact with the earth. He sees himself as grave, immovable, and silently sad (*Hombre,* p. 47). Because his appearance is so ridiculous, he is thankful for the understanding of Aretal's friends:

And I was so grateful that they finally understood me, that they did not hurt my silky feathers, that they understood my architecture of aquatic bird, that they did not find ridiculous my long bird nose, my small head bent to the front, my gray feathers and my flamingo legs!

¡Y les estaba tan agradecido de que al fin me entendieran, de que no lastimasen mis sedosas plumas, de que comprendiesen me arquitectura de ave acuática, de que no encontraran ridícula mi prolongada nariz de ave, mi pequeña cabeza inclinada hacia adelante, mi plumaje gris y mis patas de flamenco! (*Hombre,* p. 47)

Arévalo Martínez's pathetic self-portrait, besides confirming his insecurity, serves as another example of the mastery with which he is able to capture and reproduce a personality with a minimum of words. His incisive dissection of the human soul must have hurt his subjects, but they must have had to acknowledge that he was equally cruel in portraying his own feelings and failings.

IV　*"Las fieras del Trópico"*

Arévalo Martínez wrote "The Wild Beasts of the Tropics" at about the same time that he composed "The Man Who Looked Like a Horse" and "The Colombian Troubadour." Although he had intended to publish the three together, this story does not deal with the same theme. Here the author analyzes the personality of a tyrant, the dictator Estrada Cabrera. The characterization was so transparent and the political situation at that time so dangerous that the author was advised against releasing this story with the other two. This, apparently, accounts for the tale's not being published until many years later.[29]

In "The Wild Beasts of the Tropics" the psycho-zoological technique is used to portray the protagonist, but the story as a whole is rather conventional in its use of complex plot and action. The protagonist is José de Vargas, the autocratic governor of one of the states of Goldland; Mr. Ardens, a traveling cognac salesman, is the narrator. He first sees Vargas as the latter jumps onto a moving train with the easy, lithe elegance of a tiger.[30] Everyone makes way for him, and he takes a seat by the narrator, with whom he strikes up a conversation. Boldly, Ardens tells him that he has heard that he is a competent ruler, but that he is as cruel as a tiger. Vargas's offense at this observation is so marked that Ardens becomes aware of his indiscretion and, with considerable trepidation, attempts to appease the governor by referring to the nobility and beauty of a tiger. The appeasement succeeds to the extent that Vargas invites Ardens to be his guest at lunch. On arrival at the hotel, the governor pointedly ignores Ardens, devoting his entire attention to a game of billiards, but the narrator cleverly returns himself to center stage by ordering cognac for everybody in the house. This action proves to be a double triumph, for Ardens regains the attention of the governor, and the latter, impressed by the boldly subtle way in which Ardens responded to his effrontery, obliges those present to order large quantities of the cognac salesman's wares.

The lunch is interrupted by an incident between Vargas and Esquivel, one of the guests who obviously has been plotting against the governor. Vargas confronts him with the accusation, disarms him, forces him to confess all his sordid deeds in front of the other guests, and has him arrested. He is carried away by the police, but not before Vargas promises to treat him royally for as long as he behaves himself in jail. The governor then takes his leave from the guests, who remain behind and tell Mr. Ardens several anecdotes about Vargas.

Wishing to leave the country, the narrator is unsuccessful in his efforts to bid farewell to the governor. When he tries to board a train, he is informed that the governor, who wants him to remain and revise his opinion of the governor's administration, has forbidden his departure. The narrator, indeed, remains, but after learning some time later that the governor has himself killed Esquivel in prison, he knows that he must leave and begs the governor for permission to return to his young wife. The governor, moved by the narrator's romantic appeal, approves the departure and, further, removes a diamond ring from his finger and asks the narrator to take it to his wife. The narrator last sees the governor, as his train departs, stalking catlike about the station.

The delineation of the great cat is superb. He jumps onto the train with the grace and playfulness of an animal attracted by a moving object. The people around him react with admiration for his handsome bearing, but they respect his power and fear his volatile temperament. The narrator falls under the spell of his beautiful presence, forgetting for the moment the wild nature of the tiger; he soon regrets it. When he annoys Vargas by mentioning his cruelty, he unleashes the animal craft of the governor, who tries to trap him in an intellectual game of wits. Although this game is dangerous for the narrator, it is quite different from the cruel, deadly sort that Vargas will play later with Esquivel, the man who dared defy his authority. At the end, the narrator explains that he succeeds in getting away because he, being a man, understands the nature of the tiger and can manipulate the struggle in his favor. On the other hand, Esquivel, who is depicted as a bull, charges blindly without thinking and loses his life. The tiger, after all his games have been played, withdraws to lie in wait for a new prey.

Aside from the psycho-zoological study, this story is extremely interesting because, in spite of its early date of composition, it contains, in embryonic form, all the major themes that Arévalo Martínez would explore in the years to come: superb psychological analysis, attacks against the capriciousness of autocratic rule, and powerful anti-Yankee statements. Arévalo's awareness of the political situation in Guatemala indicates that his concern for social problems started much earlier than one might suspect from the analysis of his novels.

V   *"La signatura de la Esfinge"*

"The Sign of the Sphynx" (1933), subtitled "Narration of J. M. Cendal, University Professor," presents another of Arévalo Martínez's alter egos in the role of the narrator. Professor Cendal is a man who has a great degree of sensitivity for detecting the animal elements in human beings. Don Rafael uses him because he needs an extraordinarily sensitive narrator to trace this portrait, since the personality he is about to dissect is one of the most powerful he ever met. The subject, as has been mentioned before, is Gabriela Mistral, a fascinating woman whom Arévalo, as representative of his government, had occasion to meet and to escort to Lake Amatitlán on a ten day excursion when the Chilean poet visited Guatemala in 1930. The critic Carlos García Prada believes that Don Rafael penetrated her psyche with the same perceptiveness that he had brought to bear on Barba-Jacob. García Prada further suggests that, though Gabriela had the reputation of being a religious woman, one who loved children, the lowly, and the poor, those who knew her well realized that she was capable of wounding her friends and admirers with her disdainful words and her catlike pounces ("palabras desdeñosas y zarpazos de felino"), humiliating them for the pleasure of it. [31]

"The Sign of the Sphynx" has neither plot nor action; it is written as a long monologue in which the narrator tells the protagonist, Elena, how he has arrived at the conclusion that she is a lioness. The monotony of his discourse is relieved by the questions of the protagonist asking for clarification of certain points. Through Cendal's explanations to Elena, Arévalo elucidates many of his ideas about human psychology, love, and the relationship between the sexes. He also shows how his mind sharpens when trying to identify a person's double, his *nahual.*

The short story begins with Cendal's making an appointment with Elena to explain her *"signatura"* to her. Upon first seeing her, he gives the first of several physical descriptions of the woman-lioness: "I found my friend on her bed, with her handsome lioness body covered with a lounging robe; and her lionlike head, with shining and tangled hair, sunken against the sheets. Her magnificent eyes glowed in the dimness of the room" ("Encontré a mi amiga en su lecho, con su hermoso cuerpo de leona cubierto por una bata; y su leonina cabeza, de refulgente cabellera enmarañada, abatida contra las sábanas. Sus magníficos ojos fosforecían en la penumbra de la alcoba"—*Cuentos,* p. 124). Here Arévalo uses his usual technique of physical description—a well-balanced mixture of human and animal characteristics, either carefully delineated or suggested. The figure portrayed is still human, but the impression evoked in the reader is powerfully animalistic.

Elena's first question to Cendal deals with the meaning of the word *"signatura."* His answer, which offers some insight into Arévalo Martínez's psycho-zoological theories, is that the whole human race can be divided into four large groups, depending on whether their temperament is passive, passionate, intellectual, or willful. Each group is symbolized by a different animal: the ox, the lion, the eagle, and man.[32] The group ruled by man comprises the truly superior people, who through their wills are able to dominate all the rest—this was the case of the narrator in "The Wild Beasts of the Tropics," who was able to outwit all the wild beasts merely because he was the only man among them.

Another interesting point for understanding Arévalo's psycho-zoological techniques is the narrator's explanation of how the revelation of Elena's personality came to him. Don Rafael did not normally penetrate the external elements in one sudden flash,[33] and in the case of Gabriela Mistral, there were at least five visions to be integrated into the final portrait. First he perceived her strong magnetic current of vitality. Next, that she took her chess pieces with a catlike movement; then that she reminded him of a sphinx. A fourth flash came when she showed him her painting entitled "The Lion." He was finally able to put all these impressions together when he saw her, tearful and emaciated, lying on a rug. Once Cendal has been able to determine her sign, he can explain many enigmas of her personality. For example, he tells her that her fear of being too masculine is unfounded; she is intensely feminine, but with the feminity of a lioness—her strong personality frightens all but other lions away from her. Cendal explains also that the reason Elena's marriage had failed was that her husband had belonged to an inferior species of cat; he loved her, but was too weak for her. Elena's reaction to Cendal's diagnoses is one of desperation; she inquires in anguish:

—Then, is there no cure for my illness? . . .
—A lion.
—But, are there any lions left on earth?

—Entonces, ¿mi mal no tiene remedio? . . .
—Un león.
—Pero, ¿es que todavía queda algún león sobre la tierra? (*Cuentos*, p. 147)

Following the pattern of the other psycho-zoological tales, the end of this story is left open. There is no resolution, because Gabriela Mistral was still alive, and obviously, her tragedy was of such a nature that only she could resolve it; her analyst could go no further than the diagnosis of the problem.

The quick glance taken at these four tales can only hint at the richness of Arévalo Martínez's psycho-zoological world, but it certainly confirms that their importance lies in the fact that they introduce many of the themes that were to become prevalent in twentieth century literature. The author succeeds in projecting his internal visions in tangible images, creating at the same time powerful psychological studies that constitute his major contribution to Spanish American literature, a literature that until his time had concentrated on the close representation of external reality.

The psycho-zoological stories are also, in a sense, literary portraits, and as such they become a self-portrait of the artist-creator, for there is as much of the narrator in them as there is of the protagonist. Each story gives several clues to his personality, and when they are put together, they form a detailed mosaic of his character—his inferiority complex, his love of beauty, his artistic preoccupations, his search for God and self-knowledge. All of these facets of the artist are conspicuously present in the psycho-zoological tales.

VI *Other Short Stories*

Arévalo Martínez also wrote a number of short stories that have nothing to do with psycho-zoological analysis. Their style and themes, however, are still unmistakeably reflective of Arévalo's concerns. Some are outgrowths of the psycho-zoological tales; others deal with the creative process, with reincarnation, the search for God, and self-knowledge; while still others show his resentment of the misunderstandings of the critics or teach moral lessons through the use of parables.

The short stories related to "The Sign of the Sphynx" demonstrate Arévalo's propensity to keep going back to a particular subject until he was satisfied that he had elucidated it. Perhaps one of the most fascinating aspects of this short story is the narrator's reaction to the protagonist. It is possible that Gabriela Mistral was the first truly artistic, intellectual female he had ever met. Woman, in his poetry and early novels, is essential to man, but always in her role of wife and mother; in his narrative, he refers to his wife in terms of being attractive, prolific, sensible, and illiterate. Woman represented security, a kind of oasis to which he could retreat to restore his strength. Gabriela Mistral, on the other hand, was a woman of great vitality, and meeting her must have been a revelation for Don Rafael. Cendal-Arévalo writes of his mixed emotions in detail; the sexual attraction he felt for the protagonist Elena-Gabriela was strong, but he was afraid of the lioness in her personality. Arévalo's feelings were so confusing to him that he wrote several short tales trying to understand them.

For example, in "Bewitched," he tells Elena the story of his love for a Miss Unknown, admitting at the end that she is the "unknown" protagonist. Here the theme is that an artist needs to be in love with a woman in order to create his best works. He describes the meeting of their minds in terms similar to those used to explain his reaction to Barba-Jacob: because of the way she inflames him, he says, he is able to understand the universe; away from her he feels cold and unproductive.

I ended up by considering myself an electric bulb. My destiny was to burn and to shine; but I neither burned nor shined.... I lay in darkness. Suddenly some divine fingers would turn on an invisible switch and I would turn on and shine like a sun. The current, the switch, and the invisible fingers belonged to her, the heavenly magician, Miss Unknown. The current that lighted up other souls was the same that animated her own bright life. Whenever she left, I would go back to the dim life of an extinguished light bulb and to the pain of remembering the light of her presence.

Llegué a considerarme como la bombilla de una lámpara eléctrica. Mi destino era arder e iluminar; pero ni ardía, ni iluminaba... yacía en la obscuridad. De pronto unos dedos divinos movían un conmutador invisible, que daba paso a la corriente misteriosa, y yo me encendía e iluminaba como un sol. La corriente, el conmutador y los dedos invisibles provenían de ella, la maga celeste,[34] Miss Incógnita. El fluido que encendía las almas era el que animaba su propia vida encendida. Si ella se iba, yo volvía a mi opaca vida de cristal apagado y a mi pena de recordar la luz de su presencia. (*Cuentos*, pp. 155–56)

Later, Cendal explains that a woman is just as essential to the process of creation of offspring of the mind as she is for biological procreation. He believes that he has not been able to create a real masterpiece because he never had the necessary collaboration of a woman's love, but he also protests that intellectual attraction is unrelated to the physical aspects of love. This paradox worried Arévalo to the point that he wrote another story, "La Fornacina," in an effort to resolve it. In "Bewitched," however, it is clear that he could not make up his mind: first he says that true love "is total love: body and soul" ("el amor único es un amor total: el cuerpo y el alma"—*Cuentos*, p. 160), but later he asserts that "—the beautiful body of Miss Unknown could have belonged to anybody without hurting me"...." ("Aquel bello cuerpo de Miss Incógnita pudo haber sido de cualquiera sin dolerme . . ."—*Cuentos,* p. 161). Evidently Arévalo is caught here in the struggle between the spirit and the senses, a basic conflict in his nature and one of the main themes of his creative works.

"Sexual Complexity" explores that same problem and at the same time expands on another of his ideas: he believes that each soul is composed of a combination of masculine and feminine elements. He suggests that this may be because the soul has gone through a series of reincarnations, using bodies of both sexes. The more intellectually superior a person is, the more complex the sexual elements become—a condition particularly conspicuous in artists, who are extraordinarily sensitive people. Cendal believes that his close friendship with the female protagonist is due to the fact they are both artists, endowed with highly developed dual sexual characteristics that satisfy each other's needs.

I would feel comfortable in your company in times of sorrow, when every man has the soul of a child and looks for the motherliness of woman, also in times of great practicality, because woman, though so heavenly, has her feet more firmly planted on the ground than man. And I will also feel comfortable in battle, in a laboratory, and in a philosophical debate; in times of abstraction.

We have spent long hours together without boring each other. You compliment all that there is in me of man and all that there is of woman. You are at the same time my man-friend and my woman-friend.

Yo con usted me sentiría bien a la hora del dolor, en que todo varón tiene alma de niño y busca la maternidad de la mujer; a la hora de las cosas concretas, pues la mujer, tan celeste, tiene los pies más fijos en la tierra que el hombre. Y me sentiría bien en el combate, en el laboratorio y en un examen filosófico; a la hora de las abstracciones.

Hemos pasado juntos largas horas sin aburrirnos. Usted completa en mí todo lo que hay de hombre y todo lo que hay de mujer. Es a la vez el amigo y la amiga. (*Hombre,* p. 230)

But then she asks the question he has been dreading: Would he feel comfortable when it was time to make love? His answer is un-equivocal: "—At the time of love, no. In making love I would be inhibited by your cold and perpetual analysis, your cerebration, your weighing of all your actions on mental scales. Lastly, your incapacity to give of yourself in a feminine way..." ("—A la hora del amor no.

Para el amor me separa de usted su análisis frío y perpetuo, su cerebración, ese pesar de todos sus actos en balanzas mentales. En fin, su incapacidad de entrega femenina . . ."—*Hombre,* p. 232).

It was, then, her mind, her "masculine" intellect that made him admire her and consider her his equal. He could create a flood of artistic works under her influence, and yet he was incapable of making love to her. His old inferiority complex, his lack of confidence in his virility, overwhelmed him in the presence of her powerful feminine personality. He frankly admits that he does not feel comfortable with her at the time of love, but he admits just as frankly that he feels a strong sexual desire for her. The complexity of this sexual versus intellectual attraction is the subject of "La Farnecina."

"La Farnecina," subtitled "(Essay on Sexual Magic)," is structured as a series of dialogues between the poet-narrator and a male friend. He first explains that he has been deprived of his Farnecina and that he needs her presence because an ideal alone is not enough; he needs an ideal incarnated in a real woman (*Hombre,* p. 238). A woman, rather than another man, is needed because according to his theories of sexual complexity, a man does not complement another man; their opposite elements do not counterbalance each other.[35] This way of thinking makes the poet face the real question: Is his love for the Farnecina sexual? He first answers affirmatively, although he qualifies by saying that it is a sensuality of the spirit ("sensualidad del espíritu"). Despite this assertion, however, he speaks again in favor of sexual love, and when someone suggests that he loves the Farnecina like a man, he thinks:

If the light of sex did not shine, everything would be dark. Woman's attraction is a strange force, full of power. It is a mysterious polarization that transforms a man in an instant. Without this attraction, without the impact of this attraction, there would be no light. It is a magic, a formidable sorcery.

Si el sexo no encendiese sus luces todo estaría obscuro. Esta atracción de la mujer es una fuerza extraña, llena de poder. Es como una polaridad misteriosa que transforma al hombre en un minuto. Sin esta atracción, sin el choque de esta atracción, no brotaría la luz. Es una magia, un formidable hechizo. (*Hombre,* p. 256)

After several more pages of discussion, he ends the story without having arrived at a satisfactory decision: he insists that he is happy in a relationship that allows him simply to see the woman he loves. He has convinced himself not to risk losing her by trying to go beyond this.

His friend agrees that he does look content; but, he asks pointedly, are you satisfied? The narrator's answer is as ambivalent as Arévalo's feelings on this matter:

> —No. I see the Farnecina in this way; but I crave something more; I am dying of unfulfilled longing...
> —Why, when you see her often and that was all you asked for?
> —One cannot grasp the sunset...

> —No. Veo a la Farnecina en esta forma; pero ansío algo más; me muero de un deseo insaciado. . .
> —¿Por qué, si la ves y no pedías otra cosa?
> —No se puede asir el crepúsculo. . .
> (*Hombre*, p. 265)

This enigmatic answer evidently leaves the problem unresolved.

Typical of another type of concern are some short stories in which Arévalo tries to explain the creative process. "Las glándulas endocrinas" ("Endocrine Glands") is based on a personal experience that took place soon after the writing of "The Man Who Looked Like a Horse." According to his daughter Teresa, her father contracted tuberculosis, and the medicine prescribed for the illness destroyed his creative powers to the extent that he was never able to write in the same vein again[36]—or at least this is what he always believed and asserted in this short story, although to blame a medicine for his failure to create another masterpiece is an obviously simplistic rationalization. In "El hombre verde" ("The Green Man"), Arévalo sets out to determine the role of the writer in transforming an ordinary happening into an artistic tale. He concludes that this magic deed is the result of a delicate operation, carried out by an artist who consciously and carefully selects and arranges all the essential elements of the story. "La cerbatana" ("The Blowgun") is a parable in which the title symbolizes the manner in which men, and especially artists, are used by God to do His will. Men deliver their messages or do their deeds unaware that they are in reality sterile and empty blowguns, used by God for carrying out His work. The same is true of the artist, whose creations satisfy others, although they are the product of a mind only partially aware. Despite this statement, in "Una voz" ("A Voice"), he professes to be aware of the meaning of his own works. He knows exactly what he is after. Here a friend tells the narrator that all his works are marked by his desire to show that man's physical body is shaped by his spirit, and the narrator assents, but adds that he would rather say that what characterizes his works is his search for man's soul ("la búsqueda del alma"—*Monitot*, p. 167).

Perhaps one of Arévalo Martínez's favorite topics is reincarnation. He refers to his experiences with spiritualism in *The Nights at the Palace of the Nunciature*, but many of his short stories also deal with this subject. "Cratilo" ("Cratylus") is a brief tale in which Arévalo tells of having been visited in the hospital, while recuperating from an operation, by a man who called himself Nicomaco and addressed him as Cratylus. This man explained that he came bearing greetings from the dead Barba-Jacob. When Arévalo refused to believe him, the visitor gave him a copy of Plato's Cratylus and asked him to read it to see if he did not recognize himself in the protagonist. Arévalo acknowledged the similarity. "Cuento de chinos" ("A Tall Tale") is an explication of the common vague impression of having met someone before. It is revealed to the female protagonist through her dreams that in all of her several past lives she had been in some way associated with the narrator. "Los tres libros" ("The Three Books") tells of an experience similar to that used to account for *The World of the Maharachías:* through spiritualistic means, the narrator reads cabalistic books that he later finds in print.

The search for God and self-knowledge, another ever-present theme, is perhaps best exemplified by "The Man Who Looked Like a Horse." But there are several other short stories, such as "El Doctor Argentino" ("The Argentine Doctor") or "El camino real," in which the narrator tells of similar experiences. In "Mr. Monitot," Arévalo had spoken of man's need to believe in God, asserting that this need is so basic that "If a God creator of men did not exist, a God created by men would" ("si no existiera el Dios que creó a los hombres, existiría el Dios que crearon los hombres"—*Monitot*, p. 16). God is a personal need and finding Him is one of man's main concerns on Earth. "The Argentine Doctor" is, in a sense, the story of this search: the protagonist exercises a strange fascination on the narrator; he visits him assiduously, and on one occasion, the narrator observes a soft white glow emanating from the doctor's body. The news of the doctor's imminent departure shatters the narrator, but as he is taking his leave, the doctor begs him not to be upset since, as he explains, the light he had seen around him was really a reflection of the narrator's internal glow. The message in this story repeats what Arévalo Martínez had already said in "The Man Who Looked Like a Horse": the "glow" the narrator sees emanating from certain people comes from God within his own soul. "El camino real" is a parable with a similar message. A woman leads a man down a path and abandons him at a crossroad; it is night, and he is lost and alone. Then, suddenly, he finds himself in front of the home of the gods. While he waits to enter, he learns to know himself. Once inside, he realizes that if he feels at home, it is because his soul already had capacity for responding to the divine.

Another topic frequently used by Arévalo Martínez is his skepticism toward literary critics, and there are two stories that use this theme in a particularly outspoken manner. In "La esclavitud del poeta" ("The Slavery of the Poet"), he tells artists that pleasing the critics is impossible, that whoever attempts it simply becomes a slave who tries to produce jewels without brilliance and flowers without fragrance (*Monitot*, p. 195). In "La cajita" ("The Small Box") he responds to the criticism that all his psycho-zoological tales end with the departure of the protagonist. Arévalo says that his protagonists are fascinating people who have a hold on him and that the only way in which he can rid himself of their obsessive images is by sending them away. He then creates a character who is a box and who does not leave at the end, because, the author says, since it is a piece of furniture, it can stay around without bothering him.

Thematically and stylistically, Arévalo Martínez's short stories have a remarkable affinity with his poetry. They present extremely subjective visions of his internal reality; his dreams, his desires, his fears, his love for woman and God, and his eagerness to understand his role in the creation of his works are the subject matter of most of his tales. Arévalo Martínez's main contribution to Spanish American literature is precisely to have been able to take all these lyrical themes, which had traditionally been presented in the abstract language of poetry, and to recast them within the framework and language of the short story.

CHAPTER 7

Arévalo Martínez: The Innovator of Spanish American Prose-Fiction

ARÉVALO Martínez started his literary career fairly late in life. His first work, the short story "Wife and Children," was not published until 1909, when he was twenty-five years old; it was followed by his first book of poetry—*Maya* (1911); his first novel—*A Life* (1914); and his first psycho-zoological short stories—"The Man Who Looked Like a Horse," "The Colombian Troubadour," and "The Wild Beasts of the Tropics" (1914). By the time he began to write prose fiction, he was already a mature thinker and well practiced in literary technique.[1] However, though he wrote many works of value after 1914, none were to surpass the excellence of his first stories. He became known almost exclusively as the author of "The Man Who Looked Like a Horse," a fact that distressed him for the rest of his life. He blamed the medicines he had taken for his inability to produce another masterpiece, and he blamed fate for his having been born in an unknown country such as Guatemala, which prevented the wide diffusion of his works.[2] Regardless of the reasons, his early pieces of brief fiction were the most original of his works and his claim to fame rests almost exclusively on them.

All of Arévalo's narrative is extremely subjective in nature; even his political and utopian novels are presented from the point of view of an easily identifiable first person narrator. Raymond A. Moody has commented on the striking similarities of Arévalo's narrators:

> The narrator is a created character, and it is possible for an author to invent different narrators for different works, or one may say there are as many narrators as there are works. This, in Arévalo's prose, however, is not the case. In most of his stories and novels, the narrators are so much alike that it is difficult to separate them. It might be more accurate to identify them as the same. The special quality of the narrator is created in part by point of view.

118

The teller of the story tends to be the first person approximately seventy percent of the time, and the narrator talks about other people but always related to himself.[3]

The narrator, an alter ego of Arévalo Martínez, is the most important character in his works because the author found within himself the basic struggle between the spiritual and the sensual, between idealism and materialism. When Arévalo translated this struggle into ethical terms, it became the struggle between the forces of good and evil that polarized man's nature and ruled the universe. Arévalo concluded that both of these elements were essential components of the world as it exists, and that in order to survive, man must allow his rational side to prevail. The quest that brought him to this conclusion was long and two-sided. In the first place, it was metaphysical; he sought a satisfactory resolution of the conflict between his intellectual and his sensual needs. Second, Arévalo sought a solution to man's social problems and found it in a well-balanced sociopolitical atmosphere conducive to peace and harmony.

Arévalo's concerns—thematic as well as stylistic—were not typical of those expressed in the narrative of his contemporaries. He sought a high degree of artistic perfection in his writings, but unlike the early Modernists, who were interested almost exclusively in aesthetic principles, Arévalo became a committed writer. However, he re- mained a Modernist because, unlike other committed writers of his day, he did not deal with nineteenth century themes and techniques borrowed from European tradition. He was an innovator, and his revolutionary changes would open new roads. At the turn of the century, Realism, Naturalism, and *Costumbrismo* predominated in the narrative, mostly for no better reason than that they were the styles traditionally used to describe social problems and to present picturesque portraits of quaint local customs. All these modes of expression dealt with the analysis of external reality; in other words, they were limited to the physical aspects of reality. But while Spanish America continued to produce a literature still imbued with nineteenth century concepts, the rest of the Western world had embarked on an exploration of inner reality. The Symbolists, Sur- realists, Expressionists, and others introduced concepts and techniques that allowed the presentation of the world of the mind. The new reality they analyzed was not less real than the physical world described before, but it was vastly different. It differed especially in the treatment given to the characters and to point of view. In this new literature there were no longer objective standards, and all phenomena were perceived in reference to an individual and his circumstances. These changes came about gradually and with a great deal of misunderstanding from many of the critics. The change was particularly traumatic in Spanish America, where, as the Chilean novelist José Donoso affirms, even in the 1960s it was still difficult for a writer to break away from the old molds of Realism.[4]

Unknown to many, however, Arévalo Martínez, writing in the isolation of the Guatemalan highlands, had adopted the new modes of expression very early and quite independently of foreign influences, guided only by his own temperament and interests. His hypersensitive nature vibrated like a tightly strung cord with every impression and every emotion that struck his senses. The analysis of his reactions became the first subject matter of his narrative, and, with the soul of a poet, he interpreted his sensations in lyrical terms, creating new modes of expression. Since many of his feelings and thoughts were similar to those of other Spanish American writers, he was able to provide models for those who followed. For example, he found himself torn between his highly civilized European education and his concern—although at times it can rather be called contempt—for his uncivilized environment, dominated by the Indian and mixed races of the continent.[5] Arévalo presents a very subjective version of the continental struggle between civilization and barbarism, a conflict that he never completely resolved to his satisfaction. He tried to rationalize it in certain passages of *Journey to Ipanda,* but he was basically unable to accept the premise that the white and the mixed races were created equal. Despite this prejudice, his utopian novels represent a solid contribution to the eventual solution of this complex problem.

It was, perhaps, while searching for his own identity that Arévalo made his most lasting contributions to the literature of Spanish America. He searched deep in his soul and discovered that man could not understand himself without the aid of others. He then concluded that what he admired in other people was the same superior qualities that were an integral part of his own soul. Furthermore, these superior qualities were but a manifestation of the divine nature of God in man. If man partook of God's divine nature, it naturally followed that he had the ability to better himself by developing his rational faculties. Only then would man be able to create a harmonious society. Only then would the power of reason be strong enough to overcome the weaknesses inherent in human nature. It is in a sense ironic that in his quest for personal identity Arévalo Martínez became interested in social reform.

Arévalo's ideas on the self, God, and the need to develop a civilized world in order to survive are not very original. What is original is the way he expressed them. His predominant concern was the search for self-knowledge. This search is basically so subjective in nature that most creative writers who have dealt with it have traditionally been poets. The abstract and lyrical language of poetry has served them perfectly for representing their thoughts, and they have been far more skillful in expressing their ineffable feelings than Arévalo ever was in his poetry. Arévalo Martínez's claim to fame, however, comes from his successful adaptation of this poetic theme to prose fiction. He expressed his most subjective feelings in his fiction, and the entertaining accounts that emerged maintained the interest of the reader, while at the same time, if he was intellectually curious and looked below the surface, he was rewarded to find, carefully hidden under the symbols and metaphors, the true meaning of Arévalo's stories. Most of his works can be read on two levels; his best ones are like short Symbolist poems that keep revealing deeper gradations of meaning with each successive reading.

The creation of psychological novels and short stories with metaphysical dimensions is Arévalo Martínez's major contribution to Hispanic letters. His masterpiece, "The Man Who Looked Like a Horse," still stands out as one of the most provocative pieces of fiction written in the first quarter of the twentieth century. Arévalo Martínez's works successfully combined what until then had appeared in Spanish American literature as two independent currents: (1) aesthetic concerns and (2) social commitment. His narrative departs from the weary formula of the regional novel of social protest and from the type of novel that emphasized physical setting at the expense of character development. By stressing his personal search for identity and his desire to understand his place in society, Arévalo Martínez succeeded in giving a universal dimension to his creations. He led the way in the search for what was to become the most important theme of the new novelists: man's struggle to understand the role in life that fate has handed him.

Notes and References

Chapter One

1. Amy Elizabeth Jensen, *Guatemala. A Historical Survey* (New York, 1955), p. 9.

2. Nathan L. Whetten, *Guatemala. The Land and the People* (New Haven, 1961), p. 33.

3. This term refers to a type of Hispanic literature that concentrates on the description of types, manners, and milieu.

4. See Seymour Menton, *Historia crítica de la novela guatemalteca* (Guatemala City, 1960).

5. "El modernismo es la forma hispánica de la crisis universal de las letras y del espíritu que inicia hacia 1885 la disolución del siglo XIX y que se había de manifestar en el arte, la ciencia, la religión, la política y gradualmente en los demás aspectos de la vida entera, con todos sus caracteres, por lo tanto, de un hondo cambio histórico cuyo proceso continúa hoy." Federico de Onís, *Antología de la poesía española e hispanoamericana (1882–1932)* (1934; Rpt. New York, 1961), p. xv.

6. Raúl Silva Castro, "¿Es posible definir el modernismo?" *Cuadernos americanos*, 24 (1965), 172–79.

7. Juan Ramón Jiménez, *El modernismo: notas de un curso (1953)* (México, 1962).

8. Ricardo Gullón, *Direcciones del modernismo* (Madrid, 1964).

9. Ivan Schulman, *Génesis del modernismo* (México, 1966) and *El modernismo hispanoamericano* (Buenos Aires, 1969).

10. In his "Prefacio" to *Cantos de vida y esperanza* (*Songs of Life and Hope*), published in 1905, Darío states: "The movement toward freedom that I initiated in America reached as far as Spain, and both here and there its triumph is complete" ("El movimiento de libertad que me tocó iniciar en América se propagó hasta España, y tanto aquí como allá el triunfo está logrado"). Rubén Darío, *Obras poéticas completas* (Madrid, 1932), p. 831.

11. Schulman (*El modernismo*, p. 12) asserts that most of the misconceptions became prevalent only after the death of Darío, since at that time critics began to accept unquestionably Rubén's statements, forgetting to examine the literary texts and the historical facts.

12. *Ibid.*, p. 15.

13. *Ibid.*, pp. 21–22.

14. The Modernists admired certain aspects of this movement, especially its deeply felt lyrical emotion and its emphasis on musicality.

15. Arthur Rimbaud, *Poésies. Derniers vers. Une saison en enfér. Illuminations,* Daniel Leuwers, ed. ([Paris], 1972), p. 124.

16. Luis Alberto Sánchez, *La tierra del Quetzal* (Santiago de Chile, 1950), p. 165.

17. Luis Leal, *Breve historia de la novela hispanoamericana* (New York, 1971), p. 170.

18. Enrique Anderson Imbert, *La literatura hispanoamericana* (1960; Rpt. New York, 1970), II, 215.

19. Hellén Ferro, *Historia de la poesía hispanoamericana* (New York, 1964), p. 303.

20. Graciela P. de Nemes, "Literature of the Absurd," *Americas,* 17 (February 2, 1965), 6–10.

21. Kessel Schwartz, *A New History of Spanish American Fiction* (Coral Gables, Fla., 1971), II, 112.

22. Ramón Pérez de Ayala, *Amistades y recuerdos* (Barcelona, 1961), p. 300.

23. The problem of the isolation of the Latin American writer has continued until recently. José Donoso (b. 1925), the Chilean novelist, points out how difficult it was for a new artist to become known or to know what was going on beyond the borders of his country:

Before 1960 it was uncommon for nonspecialists to speak about the contemporary Spanish American novel: there were only Uruguayan and Ecuadorian novels, Mexican and Venezuelan novels. The novels of each country were known only within its borders, and their fame and relevance remained, by and large, a local matter. . . . The novelist in Spanish America wrote for his countrymen, about the problems of his countrymen, and in the language of his countrymen. . . . For those who have not known it first hand . . . it is impossible to imagine the isolation in which Spanish American novelists found themselves only ten years ago, their feeling of suffocation caused by lack of stimulus and response.

("Antes de 1960 era muy raro oír hablar de la novela hispanoamericana contemporánea a gente no especializada: existían novelas uruguayas y ecuatorianas, mexicanas y venezolanas. Las novelas de cada país quedaban confinadas dentro de sus fronteras, y su celebridad y pertinencia permanecía, en la mayor parte de los casos, asunto local. . . . El novelista de los países de Hispanoamérica escribía para su parroquia, sobre los problemas de su parroquia y con el idioma de su parroquia. . . . Para el que no lo haya vivido . . . resulta imposible imaginar la situación de aislamiento en que se encontraban los novelistas hispanoamericanos hace sólo diez años, su asfixia debido a la falta de estímulo y de eco".)

José Donoso, *Historia personal del "Boom"* (Barcelona, 1972), pp. 19–20.

24. "El caso de Osmundo Arriola," *Boletín de la Biblioteca Nacional de Guatemala,* 10 (August 1934), p. 375.

25. Carlos García Prada, ed., *Cuentos y poesías de Rafael Arévalo Martínez* (Madrid, 1961), p. 9.

26. For details pertaining to his early life and works see Teresa Arévalo,

Rafael Arévalo Martínez (Biografía de 1884 hasta 1926) (Guatemala City, 1971).

27. *Hondura* (1947; Rpt. Guatemala City, 1959), p. 104.

28. Teresa Arévalo, p. 144.

29. *Una vida: novela corta* (Guatemala City, 1914), pp. 42–44.

30. This paradoxical definition probably stemmed from the fact that Rafael obviously was intellectually gifted—thus superior—and at the same time a physical weakling, unfitted for the struggle for life—thus degenerate.

31. Teresa Arévalo, p. 106.

32. *Manuel Aldano, La lucha por la vida* (Guatemala City, 1922), pp. 14–17.

33. See *Ibid.*, ch. 64; and Federico de Onís, "Resurrección de Arévalo Martínez," *Revista de Estudios Hispánicos*, 1, no. 3 (July-September 1928), 290–95.

34. García Prada, p. 8.

35. Arturo Torres Rioseco, *Novelistas contemporáneos de América* (Santiago de Chile, 1939), p. 412.

Chapter Two

1. "I believe that in Guatemala there is no other poet who is as much a poet as Rafael Arévalo Martínez" ("Creo que no hay en Guatemala ningún poeta más hondamente poeta que Rafael Arévalo Martínez"), Santiago Argüello, Introduction to *Llama* (Guatemala City, 1934), p. 3.

2. For a detailed analysis of Arévalo's poetry see Hugo Estrada L., *La poesía de Rafael Arévalo Martínez* (Guatemala City, 1971). This critic divides the poet's works into two periods, discussed under the headings of Modernist Poetry and New Poetry.

3. *Preciosismo* derives its name from a French movement of the eighteenth century that searched for beauty in the refinement of images and expressions. By extension, it is applied to carefully affected refinement in language, style, or taste within any literary movement.

4. *Maya* (Guatemala City, 1911), p. 5.

5. Estrada L., pp. 32–35.

6. "Cánones Literarios" ("Literary Rules"), *Por un caminito así* (Guatemala City, 1947), p. 138.

7. The same concepts are expressed in an article in which he discusses what constitutes the best style: "we believe that beauty is made up of simplicity, nakedness, sobriety, and harmony. For us literary beauty is like the soft, undulating lines of a lily." See "El estilo literario," *Boletín de la Biblioteca Nacional de Guatemala*, 8, no. 3 (October 1939), 124–29.

8. *Poemas de Rafael Arévalo Martínez* (Guatemala City, 1965), p. 60.

9. The concept expressed by this image is very close to Juan Ramón Jiménez's idea that the perfection of a rose symbolizes the perfection of

poetry itself. Jiménez also felt that perfection, lest it seem artificial, always
implied a touch of imperfection, thus the thorns of the rose. The Spanish poet
put it this way: "Do not touch it any more,/for such is the rose!" ("¡No le
toques ya más,/que así es la rosa!"). *Tercera antolojía poética* (Madrid, 1957),
p. 596.

    10. In his poem "La poesía" Juan Ramón says:

> Pure, she first came to me,
> dressed in innocence:
> and I loved her as a child would.
>
> Then she started dressing
> in all sorts of clothing,
> and without knowing it, I started hating her.
>
> She became a queen,
> opulent in treasure . . .
> . . . .
> . . . Then she started undressing.
> And I smiled at her.
> . . . .
> And she removed her tunic
> and appeared all naked . . .
> Oh passion of my life, poetry,
> naked, mine forever!
>
> Vino primero, pura,
> vestida de inocencia;
> y la amé como un niño.
>
> Luego se fue vistiendo
> de no sé que ropajes;
> y la fui odiando, sin saberlo.
>
> Llegó a ser una reina,
> fastuosa de tesoros . . .
> . . . .
> . . . Mas se fue desnudando.
> Y yo la sonreía.
> . . . .
> Y se quitó la túnica
> y apareció desnuda toda . . .
> ¡Oh pasión de mi vida, poesía
> desnuda, mía para siempre!
> *Ibid*, p. 511.

    11. See Enrique González Martínez in the Prologue to *Llama* (México,
1934); Luis Alberto Sánchez, *Escritores representativos de* América, II
(Madrid, 1964); Gabriela Mistral, quoted in *Obras escogidas de Rafael*

Arévalo Martínez (Guatemala, 1959); and Carlos García Prada, Introduction to *Cuentos y poesías* (Madrid, 1961).

12. See David Vela, Prologue to *Poemas de Rafael Arévalo Martínez* (Guatemala City, 1965); and César Brañas, *Rafael Arévalo Martínez en su tiempo y en su poesía* (Guatemala City, 1946).

13. Arévalo, ch. 65, deals with the place religion and mysticism occupied in the life of her father. See also section V of Chapter 3 of this book.

14. *Los atormentados* (Guatemala City, 1914), p. 48.

15. *Las rosas de Engaddi* (San José, Costa Rica 1918), p. 14. Italics added.

Chapter Three

1. In *A New History of Spanish American Fiction*, Kessel Schwartz discusses rather thoroughly the historical and literary background of the Spanish American novel.

2. Luís Alberto Sánchez, *América; novela sin novelistas* (Santiago de Chile, 1940).

3. Ríoseco.

4. Fernando Alegría, *Breve historia de la novela hispanoamericana* (México City, 1959).

5. Magic Realism is a term created by the German critic Franz Roh in his discussion of contemporary art, principally painting. Works belonging to this modality are characterized by a highly subjective treatment of reality. The ambiguity of the words and the vagueness of the metaphors, symbols, and allegories used create a mysterious and dream-like effect in the descriptions of scenes and objects. In final analysis, although reality remains familiar and recognizable, it assumes unreal, almost fantastic dimensions.

6. Schwartz (II, 112) mentions the names of Carlos Fuentes, Julio Cortázar, Mario Vargas Llosa, and Gabriel García Márquez as examples of contemporary writers who developed themes and techniques used by Arévalo Martínez.

7. *Ibid.*, II, 112–13.

8. Menton, p. 140.

9. *Una vida* (Guatemala City, 1914), pp. 7–8.

10. In *Le petit chose*, a sentimental story, Daudet (1840–1897) told of the hardships and poverty he suffered in his early life.

11. The title of *bachiller* (high school graduate) was later changed to *poeta* after the sadistic owner discovered Aldano's literary ambitions. *Manuel Aldano: La lucha por la vida* (Guatemala City, 1922), pp. 35–36.

12. Menton, p. 140.

13. "Contribución a la preceptiva de la novela" (Speech delivered in Guatemala City, June 10, 1965), pp. 1–2. A copy of this speech was given to the present author by Don Rafael during a visit at his home in Guatemala City in the summer of 1973.

14. *Las noches en el Palacio de la Nunciatura y Sentas. The Nights* is

Arévalo's fourth novel. His third one, *La Oficina de Paz de Orolandia* (1925), grew out of the same political concerns the author had shown in the last section of *Manuel Aldano*. Because of its theme, its significance will be discussed in Chapter 4, together with other works of social commitment.

15. Schwartz, II, 113.

16. The relationship between Sentas and the narrator is partially autobiographical; it is based on Arévalo's love affair with Amalia Quinteros. Their engagement was broken by his mother, who forbade him to marry on the grounds that he was too weak to provide for a family. Arévalo, pp. 165–70.

17. Emanuel Swedenborg (Sweden, 1688–1772) was a scientist, inventor, and mystical religious leader. He wrote a number of books setting forth what he called his "heavenly doctrines." He claimed that they had been revealed to him through direct communication with the spiritual world.

18. Anna Balakian, *The Symbolist Movement: A Critical Appraisal* (New York, 1967), p. 12.

19. See *4 contactos con lo sobrenatural y otros relatos* (Guatemala City, 1971), pp. 48–70.

20. John Senior, *The Way Down and Out: The Occult in Symbolist Literature* (Ithaca, New York, 1959), p. xxi.

21. *Ibid.*, p. 8.

22. The same concepts had been discussed by Manuel Aldano in his conversation with Dr. Esquerdo. *Aldano*, pp. 109–16.

23. *Las noches en el Palacio de la Nunciatura* (Guatemala City, 1927), pp. 8–9.

24. Arévalo, pp. 343–46.

25. Arévalo Martínez breaks quite a number of conventions by the mere mention of homosexuality. According to Alberto Zum Felde, *Índice crítico de la literatura hispanoamericana: II La narrativa* (México City, 1959), he is the first author to introduce this theme in Spanish American literature (p. 493).

26. Aretal's homosexuality is not discussed by Arévalo Martínez in this book, but he has mentioned it in other works, and it would have been known to any reader of Arévalo's works, either at the time of publication of *The Nights*, or today. For a full explanation of Aretal, his identity, and his relationship with Arévalo Martínez, see Chapter 6.

27. Aldano's wife is described as an illiterate and prolific woman, one with whom intellectual communion would be impossible. Rafael Arévalo Martínez explains his affinity for Plato's ideas in "Cratilo," *Cratilo y otros cuentos* (Guatemala City, 1968) and in "Nicòmaco," *4 contactos con lo sobrenatural y otros relatos*.

Chapter Four

1. Raymond A. Moody, "The Life and Prose Style of Rafael Arévalo Martínez" (Ph.D. dissertation, UCLA, 1967), p. 449.

2. See Chapter 3, pp. 00–00.

3. Menton, p. 140.

4. Thomas E. Holland, "The United States in Twentieth Century Guatemalan Literature" (Ph.D. dissertation, USC, 1968), p. 77.

5. Schwartz, II, 115.

6. Arévalo, pp. 339–42, 413–14.

7. Holland, p. 81. This opinion is shared by Menton, p. 143.

8. *La Oficina de Paz de Orolandia, Novela del imperialismo yanqui* (Guatemala City, 1925), p. 115.

9. Identified by the critics as Manuel Ugarte (Argentina, 1878–1951), a novelist and essay writer who coined the phrase "Colossus of the North."

10. Arévalo Martínez explains that the importance of this biography is that the protagonist can be studied as the prototype of any Latin American dictator. ¡*Ecce Pericles!* (Guatemala City, 1971), I, 81.

11. One of the few funny incidents in the book deals with these festivals. One year they coincided with large-scale volcanic activity, but Estrada Cabrera would not even allow nature to interfere with his pet project. He simply issued an edict assuring the people that the eruptions were taking place in Mexico. The edict was read at noon, but by the light of a lantern due to the darkness caused by the ashes and rock falling all around the soldiers and the frightened people, who could barely remain still while the earth shook under their feet (*Ecce*, I, 91–92).

12. The closest he comes to an accusation is in reference to an American envoy called McMillin of whom Arévalo Martínez says that he was popularly known as *sacacorchos* ("corkscrew") because he was used by the United States for removing Latin American presidents from office.

13. They are also like many of the incidents told by Miguel Angel Asturias in *El señor presidente*.

14. *Hondura*, p. 75.

15. Schwartz, II, 116.

Chapter Five

1. Joseph L. Love, "Utopianism in Latin American Cultures," in *Aware of Utopia* (Urbana, Ill., 1971), p. 117.

2. *Ibid.*, p. 118.

3. *El mundo de los maharachías* (Guatemala City, 1939), p. 8.

4. See Vasconcelos' *La raza cósmica* (1925) and *Indología* (1926) and Rojas' *Eurindia* (1942).

5. *Viaje a Ipanda* (Guatemala City 1939), p. 9.

6. His ideas on this particular point correspond quite closely to those presented by José Enrique Rodó in *Ariel* (1900).

7. The name "Gracia" seems to be a combination of Grecia and Francia. As a Modernist, Arévalo Martínez revered France and the vision of Greece as

seen through the French writers of the nineteenth century. Hernón says: "Gracia represents freedom and light. A true descendent of Elena, it lives in full day light and avoids the darkness of the dusk" ("Gracia representa la libertad y la luz. Descendiente legítima de Elena, vive en pleno medio día y huye de la penumbra crepuscular".) And later on he adds: "I am a Gracian more than an Ipandian. I—and my now old generation with me—were nursed at the breast of Gracia rather than by Ipanda" ("Yo soy más que ipandés graciano. Yo—y conmigo mi generación, ya vieja hoy—nos amamantamos a los pechos de Gracia más que a los de Ipanda"—*Viaje*, pp. 157–58).

8. Prologue to *El embajador de Torlania*, Pedro Arce Valladares,— (Guatemala City, 1960), pp. 38–39.

9. Arévalo Martínez seems to have been fascinated by Decio's lover. Years after *The Ambassador from Torlania*, he published a short story, "Mrs. Ferguson," in which he elaborated on her character and recounted what became of her after the ambassador's assassination.

10. *El embajador de Torlania* (Guatemala City, 1960), p. 80.

11. Joyce Oramel Hertzler, *The History of Utopian Thought* (New York, 1923), p. 2.

12. "*Arcadia* and its variants—golden age, Thebaid, pastoral settings— express the return to a time free from social restraints. Arcadia is a country where the individual is king and where relations are carried out in absolute openness, to the slow rhythm of a life that tries to harmonize with natural and cosmic life. Arcadia makes a social law out of individual desire, assuming more or less consciously the natural goodness of man. . . . Arcadia is the return to nature: a nature that has not been marred by the creation of cities and that gives rise to a life where commercial and industrial activities do not exist. In the economic meaning of the word, it is a 'return to the land,' with all its implications of frugality, of simplicity. . . ." Claude G. Dubois, *Problèmes de l'utopie*, Archives de Lettres Modernes, Num. 85 (Paris, 1968), p. 5.

Chapter Six

1. Alegría, p. 131.

2. Chris L. Dubs, "Characterization in the Prose Fiction of Rafael Arévalo Martínez" (Ph.D. dissertation, University of Kentucky, 1972), p. 18.

3. Damián Carlos Bayón, "*Platero y yo y Españoles de tres mundos*," *La Torre*, 19–20 (July-December 1957), 374. The critic says "the character *is seen all at once*, in a circumstance that could be any other, but that is chosen by the author as being *significative of the total*, since it is used as a point of departure for building the portrait" ("el personaje *está visto de una vez*, en una circunstancia que pudo ser cualquiera, pero que el autor escoge como *significativa total*, ya que a partir de ella construye el retrato").

4. Alberto R. Lopes, "Rafael Arévalo Martínez y su ciclo de animales," *Revista Iberoamericana*, 4 (1924), 324.

5. Dubs, p. 12.

6. *Ibid.*, p. 70.

7. In *Manual Aldano* and several short stories Arévalo Martínez mentions his own ability to perceive the animal in people. In other stories he refers to a Professor Cenobio, whose ability was greater; he did not stop at simply seeing the animal in man, he could also distinguish the various species of animals.

8. The critic Fernando Alegría concurs with this interpretation (p. 131): "The Indians of his country believe that everyone has a double that accompanies him, visibly or invisibly, throughout his whole existence and that the double—an animal—partakes of the very essence of his life" ("Los indios de su tierra creen que todo hombre posee un doble que le acompaña, visible o invisiblemente, a través de toda su existencia y que ese doble—un animal—participa de la esencia misma de su vida").

9. This interpretation of the psycho-zoological stories is supported by the fact that in *The World of the Maharachías* Arévalo Martínez explains that when Aixa lost her tail, she also lost her sense of the earth, her communion with the higher forces of the universe, bringing about the downfall of Maharachían civilization.

10. Another Guatemalan author who uses the *nahual* in his works is Miguel Angel Asturias. In several of his works he points out the importance of the mythical *nahual* and how the loss of primitive beliefs affects the lives of contemporary Indians. See *Leyendas de Guatemala* (1933), *Hombres de maíz* (1954), and *Mulata de tal* (1963).

11. Barba-Jacob is one of the pseudonyms used by the notoriously decadent Colombian poet Miguel Angel Osorio. Other pen names are Ricardo Arenales and Maín Ximénez. See Arévalo, p. 255.

12. *El hombre que parecía un caballo y otros cuentos* (Guatemala City, 1951), p. 14.

13. Quoted by Zum Felde, p. 492.

14. *Juicios sobre Rafael Arévalo Martínez y lista de sus obras* (Guatemala City, 1959), p. 19.

15. *Ibid.*, pp. 20–21.

16. *Ibid.*, p. 21.

17. *Ibid.*, p. 26.

18. Arévalo, p. 269.

19. Teresa Arévalo explains that, ironically, despite Barba-Jacob's protestations, "he was quick to claim that he was the protagonist in every country he visited. . . ." ("se apresuró a proclamar que él era el protagonista en todos aquellos países a donde llegó. . ."—*Ibid.*, p. 280).

20. Moody, p. 359.

21. Quoted by Arévalo, p. 281.

22. Daniel R. Reedy, "La dualidad del 'yo' en 'El hombre que parecía un caballo'," in *El ensayo y la crítica en Iberoamérica*. Memorias del XIV Congreso Internacional de la Literatura Iberoamericana (Toronto, 1970), p. 168.

23. "Porfirio Barba-Jacob," *4 contactos con lo sobrenatural y otros relatos* pp. 53–58.

24. Quoted by Joseph Anthony Lonteen, *Interpretación de una amistad intelectual y su producto literario: El hombre que parecía un caballo* (Guatemala City, 1968), p. 71.

25. *4 contactos*, p. 57.

26. *Ibid.*

27. See Chapter 3 of this book.

28. Arévalo's mixture of neomysticism and pantheistic search makes it possible to compare him again to Juan Ramón Jiménez. The Spanish poet expressed a similar discovery in one of his best-known poems (p. 1014):

> But you god, you also are in this depth
> . . . . : . . . .
> which is my own sacred depth
>   And you were in this well before
> with the flower, with the swallow, the bull
> and the water . . .

> Pero tu dios también estás en este fondo
> . . . .
> que es el fondo sagrado de mi mismo
>   Y en este pozo estabas antes tú
> con la flor, con la golondrina, el toro
> y el agua . . .

29. Preliminary note to "Las fieras del trópico," *El señor Monitot* (Guatemala City, 1922).

30. In Spanish America, the word *tigre* normally means "jaguar," and several critics translate it that way in this story. In my opinion, however, the author really meant tiger. There are several allusions to India and Bengal tigers; besides, the sensuousness, beauty, and elegance embodied in this animal, plus his traditional and legendary cruelty, are the very essence of Vargas' characterization. The jaguar simply does not suggest the same qualities with equal force.

31. *Cuentos y poesías*, Introdución, selecciones y notas de Carlos García Prada (Madrid, 1961), pp. 123–24.

32. It is interesting to note that Arévalo places at the head of each group the four animals that symbolize the four Evangelists—Mathew, Mark, Luke, and John—which in turn are taken from the descriptions done by John (Apocalypse, 4:7) and Ezekiel (1:10) of the four living beings who support the throne of the Almighty.

33. Cendal explains also that sometimes it is possible to miss the mark because "on every man there is a mantle that covers his hieroglyphic, a fabric that cloaks the animal and is very difficult for the spectator to penetrate with

the eyes of the soul in order to see the covered beast" ("en todo hombre hay una capa que encubre su hieroglífico, una tela que viste al animal, y cuesta al espectador atravesarla con los ojos del alma y ver a la bestia encubierta"— *Cuentos,* p. 130).

34. *Celeste* is a difficult word to translate, since in Spanish it means heavenly and sky blue. Furthermore, according to Arévalo's symbolism in "The Man Who Looked Like a Horse," blue is the color of purity, of his soul, and of God.

35. This conclusion seems to be at odds with the fact that he had attained some sort of mystical union with Barba-Jacob. Perhaps the fact that the Colombian writer was a homosexual might have entered into the picture in reference to the masculine-feminine elements needed for counterbalancing each other's needs.

36. Arévalo, p. 373.

Chapter Seven

1. Raymond A. Moody, after analyzing Arévalo's style, reaches the conclusion that "most of the basic stylistic features of Arévalo's prose are present from the very first, although the full exploitation of some elements did not develop until later" (p. 448).

2. Arévalo Martínez referred several times to the handicap of being born in Spanish America and of having to write in Spanish. He has even commented on the French writer Simone de Beauvoir's sarcastic words: "To be the greatest writer of Guatemala or Honduras, what a joke!" ("Ser el más grande escritor de Guatemala o de Honduras, ¡qué risible!"). Quoted by Pedro Arce Valladares in the prologue to *El embajador de Torlania,* p. 31.

3. Moody, p. 365.

4. In reference to the persistent and negative effects of Realism in Spanish American literature, Donoso (p. 23) has said that the Realists "catalogued the flora and the fauna, the races and the expressions that are unmistakably ours, and a novel was considered *good* if it reproduced faithfully those indigenous worlds, that which specifically *made us different*—isolated us—from other regions and other countries in the continent: a kind of indestructible chauvinistic machismo" ("fueron catalogando la flora y la fauna, las razas y los dichos inconfundiblemente nuestros, y una novela era considerada *buena* si reproducía con fidelidad esos mundos autóctonos, aquello que específicamente nos *diferenciaba*—nos separaba—de otras regiones y de otros países del continente: una especie de machismo chauvinista a toda prueba"). This way of writing was accepted by the critics and considered the only way for a Latin American to write. The adherence to these standards established, according to Donoso, (p. 24) "one of the rules of literary taste that has hurt the Spanish American novel most and that is still applied by those who are not very well informed: that exactness in portraying our things, the demonstrable verisimilitude that

transforms a novel into a document that faithfully portrays or reproduces a segment of uniform reality, is the only true criterion of excellence" ("uno de los cánones del gusto literario que más daño ha hecho a la novela hispanoamericana y que los no muy avisados todavía aplican: que la *precisión* para retratar las cosas nuestras, la verosimilitud comprobable que tiende a transformar a la novela en un documento fiel que retrata o recoge un segmento de la realidad unívoca, es el único, el verdadero criterio de excelencia").

5. In reference to the tragic struggle between civilization and barbarism that divides Spanish American culture, Arévalo said:

The tragedy of the Spanish American—except in a few centers of population—in my opinion, is the following: as a member of the upper class, he inherits all the treasure of civilization. . . . [But] the environment in which he lives does not harmonize with this refined culture: the environment is, by and large, savage and barbaric. . . . Then, the Spanish American, upon attaining intellectual maturity, finds himself beset by two dissimilar forces: one, his heritage, his cultural tradition, the civilization incorporated into his Aryan blood; the other, the savage environment that surrounds him. He is continuously forced to choose between being victim or executioner, opposite extremes from which a superior, well-organized society is supposed to free us.

La tragedia del hispanoamericano—salvo en contados nucleos de población—a mi entender, es la siguiente: en las clases altas hereda todo el tesoro de la civilización. . . . Por el medio en que vive no coincide con esta tradición de cultura: el medio en gran parte, sigue siendo salvaje y bárbaro. . . . Entonces el hispamerio, al llegar a la madurez intelectual, se siente solicitado por dos fuerzas distintas: una, la de su abolengo, la de su tradición cultural, la de la civilización incorporada a su sangre aria; otra, la del ambiente bárbaro que lo rodea. Continuamente se ve en el caso de elegir entre ser víctima o verdugo, esos dos extremos opuestos, de los que precisamente está llamada a librarnos una comunidad superior, bien organizada.

"Novelas americanas," *Boletín de la Biblioteca Nacional de Guatemala*, I, 3 (November 1933). 84.

Selected Bibliography

PRIMARY SOURCES

1. Principal Works of Rafael Arévalo Martínez

Los atormentados. Guatemala City: Editorial Unión Tipográfica Gutiérrez, 1914.

Concepción del cosmos. El acertijo del mundo no tiene solución. Guatemala City: Editorial Landívar, 1954.

Cratilo y otros cuentos. Guatemala City: Editorial Universitaria, 1968.

4 contactos con lo sobrenatural y otros relatos. Guatemala City: Editorial Landívar, 1971.

Los Duques de Endor. Guatemala City: Talleres de la Imprenta del "Centro Editorial," 1940.

¡Ecce Pericles! Prólogo de Julio Bianchi. Guatemala City: Tipografía Nacional, 1945.

El embajador de Torlania. Prologue by Pedro Arce Valladares. Guatemala City: Editorial Landívar, 1960.

El hijo pródigo. Guatemala: Tipografía Nacional, 1956.

El hombre que parecía un caballo. Quetzaltenango: Tipografía Arte Nuevo, 1915.

El hombre que parecía un caballo y otros cuentos. Guatemala City: Editorial Universitaria, 1951.

Hondura. Guatemala City: Folletín del diario *La Hora*, 1947.

Influencia de España en la formación de la nacionalidad centroamericana. Guatemala City: Tipografía Nacional, 1943.

Llama. Prólogo de Enrique González Martínez. Mexico City: Imprenta Mundial, 1934.

Llama y El Rubén poseído por el deus. Guatemala City: Editorial Librería Renacimiento, 1934.

Manuel Aldano. La lucha por la vida. Guatemala City: Talleres "Gutenberg," 1922.

Maya. Prólogo de José Santos Chocano. Guatemala City: Tipografía Sánchez & de Guise, 1911.

Narración sumaria de mi vida. Guatemala City: Editorial Landívar, 1968.

El mundo de los maharachías. Guatemala City: Unión Tipográfica. Muñoz Plaza y Cía., 1939.

Nietzsche el conquistador. La doctrina que engendró la segunda guerra mundial. Guatemala City: Tipografía Sánchez & de Guise, 1943.

135

Las noches en el Palacio de la Nunciatura y Sentas. Guatemala City: Tipografía Sánchez & de Guise, 1927.

La Oficina de Paz de Orolandia. Novela del imperialismo yanqui. Guatemala City: Tipografía Sánchez & de Guise, 1925.

Por un caminito así. Guatemala City: Unión Tipográfica Castañeda, Avila y Cía., 1947.

Las rosas de Engaddi. San José, Costa Rica: Biblioteca Renovación, 1918.

El señor Monitot. Guatemala City: Editorial Sánchez & de Guise, 1922.

La signatura de la esfinge. Narración de J. M. Cendal, Profesor universitario y El hechizado. Guatemala City: Imprenta Electra, 1933.

Una vida: Novela corta. Guatemala City: Imprenta Electra, 1914.

Viaje a Ipanda. Prólogo de Federico Hernández de León. Guatemala City: Centro Editorial, 1939.

2. Anthologies and Collections

Cuentos y poesías. Ed. Carlos García Prada. Madrid: Ediciones Iberoamericanas, 1966. A good introduction.

Obras escogidas. Prólogo de Carlos Martínez Durán. Guatemala City: Editorial Universitaria, 1959.

Poemas: Febrero 1909–Febrero 1959. Guatemala City: Editorial Landívar, 1958.

Poemas. Guatemala City: Editorial José de Pineda Ibarra, 1965.

Poemas de Rafael Arévalo Martínez. Prólogo de David Vela. Guatemala City: Tipografía Nacional, 1965.

Poesías escogidas. Guatemala City: Editorial "El Sol," 1921.

SECONDARY SOURCES

ARÉVALO, TERESA. *Rafael Arévalo Martínez (Biografía de 1884 hasta 1926).* Guatemala City: Tipografía Nacional, 1971. A detailed biography of the first half of her father's life. She clarifies dates of composition, sources of inspiration, and other biographical details mentioned in her father's works.

BRAÑAS, CÉSAR. *Rafael Arévalo Martínez en su tiempo y en su poesía.* Guatemala City: Unión Tipográfica, 1946. A general introduction to Arévalo's poetry, with a rather personal approach.

DUBS, CHRIS LEE. "Characterization in the Prose Fiction of Rafael Arévalo Martínez." Ph.D. dissertation, University of Kentucky, 1972. An unpublished doctoral thesis wherein the author analyzes Arévalo's techniques of characterization, especially in the psycho-zoological narrative.

ESTRADA L., HUGO. *La poesía de Rafael Arévalo Martínez.* Guatemala City: Tipografía Nacional, 1971. A thesis written at the University of San Carlos, Guatemala. It is the most thorough study of Arévalo's poetry available.

HOLLAND, THOMAS EDWARD. "The United States in Twentieth Century

Guatemalan Literature." Ph.D. dissertation, USC, 1968. Analysis of the United States as a theme in the literature of Guatemala. The author dedicates a section to Arévalo's anti-imperialistic novels.

Juicios sobre Rafael Arévalo Martínez y lista de sus obras. 1909—febrero— 1959. Guatemala City: Editorial del Ministerro de Educación Pública, 1959. Presents an useful collection of critical commentaries. The list of publications, although incomplete, is helpful for identifying many of Arévalo's articles published in minor periodicals.

LONTEEN, JOSEPH ANTHONY. *Interpretación de una amistad intelectual y su producto literario: El hombre que parecía un caballo.* Guatemala City: Editorial Landívar, 1968. Originally a master's thesis submitted to Illinois State University. It analyzes Arévalo's and Barba-Jacob's friendship, the writing of "El hombre que parecía un caballo," and some of the resulting polemics and reactions.

LOPES, ALBERTO R. "Rafael Arévalo Martínez y su ciclo de animales." *Revista Iberoamericana,* 4 (1942), 323–31. An introduction to Arévalo's unsettling animal world.

MENTON, SEYMOUR. *Historia crítica de la novela guatemalteca.* Guatemala City: Editorial Universitaria, 1960. Menton studies Arévalo in the section dedicated to the Modernist novel.

MOODY, RAYMOND ALBERT. "The Life and the Prose Style of Rafael Arévalo Martínez." Ph.D. dissertation, UCLA, 1967. A general study of his prose with an excellent bibliography.

NEMES, GRACIELA PALAU DE. "Literature of the Absurd." *Americas,* 17 (February 2, 1965), 6–10. Analysis of the psycho-zoological tale as a precursor of the literature of the absurd.

ONÍS, FEDERICO DE. "Resurrección de Arévalo Martínez." *Revista de Estudios Hispánicos.* 1, no. 3 (July-September 1928), 290–95. He comments also on the lack of information available about Latin American writers and news.

Rafael Arévalo Martínez. Homenaje. Perfil biográfico y bibliográfico por Gonzalo Dardón Córdova. Guatemala City: Instituto Guatemalteco-Americano, 1959. A brief biography and list of publications, commemorating Arévalo's golden anniversary in his literary profession.

REEDY, DANIEL R. "La dualidad del 'yo' en 'El hombre que parecía un caballo'." In *El ensayo y la crítica literaria en Iberoamérica,* pp. 167–74. Toronto: Universidad de Toronto, 1970. A study of "The Man Who Looked Like a Horse" showing the dual personality of the narrator.

SÁNCHEZ, LUIS ALBERTO. *La tierra del Quetzal.* Santiago de Chile: Ediciones Ercilla, 1950. The chapter entitled "Arévalo Martínez, el sonámbulo" is a brief introduction to the literary world of the Guatemalan writer.

Index